SIGNING
FOR
KIDS

Eben Zamora   Mickey Flodin

A PERIGEE BOOK

A PERIGEE BOOK
Published by Penguin Group (USA) Inc.
375 Hudson Street, New York, New York 10014, USA
Penguin Group (Canada), 90 Eglinton Avenue East, Suite 700, Toronto, Ontario M4P 2Y3, Canada
(a division of Pearson Penguin Canada Inc.)
Penguin Books Ltd., 80 Strand, London WC2R 0RL, England
Penguin Group Ireland, 25 St. Stephen's Green, Dublin 2, Ireland (a division of Penguin Books Ltd.)
Penguin Group (Australia), 250 Camberwell Road, Camberwell, Victoria 3124, Australia
(a division of Pearson Australia Group Pty. Ltd.)
Penguin Books India Pvt. Ltd., 11 Community Centre, Panchsheel Park, New Delhi—110 017, India
Penguin Group (NZ), Cnr. Airborne and Rosedale Roads, Albany, Auckland 1310, New Zealand
(a division of Pearson New Zealand Ltd.)
Penguin Books (South Africa) (Pty.) Ltd., 24 Sturdee Avenue, Rosebank, Johannesburg 2196, South Africa

Penguin Books Ltd., Registered Offices: 80 Strand, London WC2R 0RL, England

While the author has made every effort to provide accurate telephone numbers and Internet addresses
at the time of publication, neither the publisher nor the author assumes any responsibility for errors,
or for changes that occur after publication. Further, the publisher does not have any control over and
does not assume any responsibility for author or third-party websites or their content.

PRINTING HISTORY
Perigee trade paperback first edition / 1991
Perigee trade paperback expanded edition / January 2007

Perigee expanded edition ISBN: 978-0-399-53320-4

The Library of Congress has cataloged the first Perigee edition as follows:

Flodin, Mickey.
Signing for kids / Mickey Flodin.
p.   cm.
Includes index.
Summary: An introduction to the expressive language of the deaf,
organized by subject areas, including Pets, People, Numbers, Sports,
Travel, Science, Thoughts and Feelings, and Places.
ISBN 0-399-51672-7
1. Sign language—Juvenile literature.   [1. Sign language.]
I. Title.
HV2476.F58   1991   90-27055   CIP   AC
419—dc20

PRINTED IN THE UNITED STATES OF AMERICA
10 9 8 7 6 5

Most Perigee Books are available at special quantity discounts for bulk purchases for sales promotions,
premiums, fund-raising, or educational use. Special books, or book excerpts, can also be created to fit
specific needs. For details, write: Special Markets, The Berkley Publishing Group, 375 Hudson Street,
New York, New York 10014.

Acknowledgments

Each of the following people has contributed uniquely to *Signing for Kids*. Without their help, I would have been at a great loss. A heartfelt thank you to:

Gene Brissie, former publisher, Perigee Books, for his enthusiasm, foresight, and determination to publish a much-needed sign-language book designed especially for kids.

Karen Twigg, for her willingness to offer valuable suggestions and tips on various aspects of *Signing for Kids*. Karen is a dear friend who has had twenty-two years' experience teaching and interpreting sign language. She has taught deaf people and conducted classes for interpreters, and has used her skills in schools, courtrooms, hospitals and churches. Karen studied interpreting at the University of Akron, in Ohio; earned her BA and MS in education at Southwest Missouri State University, in Springfield, Missouri; and taught sign language at Baptist Bible College, also in Springfield. She has been included in *Who's Who in American Education* for 1989-1990, as a classroom educator. Although she is very busy, Karen found time to give insightful advice, for which I am grateful.

Carol Flodin, my companion and best friend, who has been a part of this book from the beginning. Together we developed the original plan for the book six years ago, and since then Carol has worked with me on all aspects of the book—typing, cutting out illustrations of signs, finding models and making suggestions in the manuscript. Thanks, honey, for all your help.

Rod Butterworth, my good friend, for allowing me to use written descriptions from our three sign-language books.

All of the kids who modeled for the pictures. They were a fun bunch to photograph. The models are, in alphabetical order, Melissa Armstrong, Daniel Flodin, Ana Rusk, Elisabeth Rusk and Wesley Young.

Daniel Flodin, who completed most of the paste-up work himself and helped in many other areas—not least of which was the title of the book. "Why not call it *Signing for Kids?*" he said. And so it has become.

To a great kid,
whose creative imagination seems
to know no bounds
and who brings me great joy,
my son,
Daniel

Contents

Introduction

Just imagine being able to "talk" with your hands. Well, that's what *Signing for Kids* is all about: learning the expressive language of deaf people known as American Sign Language. It's a language that uses facial expressions, gestures, body language and manual signs to "talk." You'll have lots of fun not only learning to sign, but also "talking" to your friends and family with your hands.

Many people learn sign language because they are deaf or know someone who is. If you have a deaf friend or relative, *Signing for Kids* will help you "talk" to them and express your thoughts and feelings.

And since technology is a major part of our everyday lives, a new chapter of computer and technology signs has been added to this expanded edition to help you sign even more concepts.

When I was a boy, I met a distant cousin who is deaf. I had never been around a deaf person before and didn't know what to do or how to act. I tried talking to her, but she couldn't hear what I was saying. This became very frustrating for both of us. No matter what we did, we could not talk together or communicate. When she signed, I did not understand. When I spoke, she could not hear. But I was amazed to see her "talking" with her hands. She must be very smart to know how to do that, I thought. How I wanted to communicate with her and become better friends. But I couldn't because I didn't know her language. I hope that if you have a deaf friend or relative, you will not experience the frustration we felt. At the time, I didn't know of any books to learn her language. How I wish a book such as this had been available then. This is one of the reasons *Signing for Kids* has been written.

If you don't know anyone deaf right now, don't let that stop you from learning this expressive and beautiful language. Thousands of people are learning to sign simply because it's a lot of fun.

Just think of the possibilities for using sign language. You could sign a "secret" message to a friend across a crowded room, a quiet library or at a noisy sports arena. You can even sign underwater. One of the most expressive ways to use sign language is signing to music. Many signed music performances are given each year, so why not learn to sign your favorite song? Most of all, you will be learning the language of approximately half a million deaf people in the United States.

How to Use This Book

Each of the eighteen chapters in *Signing for Kids* deals with a special area of interest; chapter one, for instance, teaches you signs related to pets and other animals. Although it is recommended that you learn all the signs in a chapter before moving on to the next, it is not necessary. You can skip from one chapter to another, finding signs to express your thoughts to your family and friends. The book has been divided into the various sections because many of the signs in a given chapter are related to one or more similar subjects, have similar movements and are easier to learn together. Also included are several games for you to enjoy.

The Manual Alphabet and Fingerspelling

One of the first things you will want to learn is the manual alphabet on page 10. Each letter of the alphabet is represented by a hand shape. With the manual alphabet you can spell out words whose sign you don't know or words that have no formal signs—for example, names of people, places and technical terms. Many of the manual alphabet hand shapes look like the printed letters of the English alphabet, so they are easy to remember. Such as C, I, L, O, V and W. For more information on finger-spelling, see page 15.

Sign Directions

Most of the signs are shown as you would see someone signing to you. Some signs are shown close up or from an angle or profile view to make them easier to understand. Remember to face the person you are signing with. Look at the arrows and written descriptions closely for the direction and movement of the sign. When instructions are given to move the hands or fingers clockwise or counterclockwise, it is from the viewpoint of the signer (as if looking at a clock), not from the viewpoint of someone watching.

Tips to Make Signing Easier

The Signing Area

Most signs are made within an imaginary rectangle in front of the body. This area extends from shoulder to shoulder and from the top of the head to the waist, with the majority of signing being formed near the head, face and neck. Many two-handed signs are done in the chest area.

Signing Area

Right or Left Hand?

The signs in this book were drawn for right-handed people. If you are left-handed, don't worry; just use your left hand and reverse the sign. If you use both hands equally well, use the hand that is more comfortable for you.

Male and Female Signs

Many male signs are made near the forehead, while many female signs are made near the lower part of the cheek or chin. See *aunt* and *uncle* at right. Remembering this will help you learn male and female signs more quickly.

Uncle

Initialized Signs

As you begin to learn signing, you will notice that many signs are "initialized." What does this mean? The term refers to a sign formed with the fingerspelled hand shape of the first letter of the English word. An example is the sign for *family*: it is made with two *F* hands (page 30). Other examples are *rocket* and *universe* on page 110.

Aunt

More than One (Plurals)

In signing, plural forms for words are normally not needed. The context in which a sign is used will indicate whether it is singular or plural. Plurals can be signed in

a few ways when they are needed. One way is to add a sign for a number or quantity, such as *seven turtles* or, *many turtles*. Another way is to repeat the sign two or three times: repeating the sign for *bicycle* means "many bicycles." The last way is to make a sign and point in the air at different places: if you sign *rabbit* and point to different places, the meaning is "many rabbits."

Questions and Punctuation

A quizzical or questioning look and body language will help get it across that you are asking a question. Holding the last sign of a sentence a little longer helps too. You may add the question mark (page 155) at the beginning or end of a question, if you like. To indicate the end of a thought or sentence, just pause for a moment.

The *Person Ending* Sign

This sign usually relates to a person's occupation, position in life or nationality. It is used after another sign. For example, signing *art* and the *person* ending means "artist"; signing *farm* and the *person* ending means "farmer"; and signing *America* and the *person* ending means "American."

Person Ending

Past, Present and Future Time

Indicating past, present and future time with signs may be easier if you think of the area immediately in front of your body as representing present time. Signs for present time, such as *today* and *now*, are made in front of the body. Signs dealing with the future, such as *tomorrow* and *forever*, are made with a forward movement from the body. Signs about the past, such as *yesterday* and *past*, are done with a backward movement.

Thinking and Feeling Signs

Signs that deal with thinking or mental activity are usually made at or near the head. An example is *idea*. Another group of signs are those that deal with feelings. Many of these signs are done in the chest area near or at the heart, such as *happy*.

Happy

Signing Negatives

Signers can show the negative by signing *not*, or simply shake the head back and forth to signify "no" and omit the sign for *not*. Example: If you sign *not* and *like* it becomes *dislike* or *don't like*. Making the sign for *want* and shaking the head "no" means *don't want*.

Getting Someone's Attention

Starting a conversation with a deaf person is different from starting a conversation with a hearing person. In spoken language, you can begin a conversation with someone who is not looking at you. In sign language you must get the person's visual attention. You can do this by looking them in the eyes, tapping the person on the shoulder or touching the person's arm. When signing with a deaf person, it is important to maintain eye contact. If you look away, they will think the conversation has ended.

You Can Do It

Now that you know the basics, have fun "talking" with your hands to your family and friends. Sometimes you may forget a sign or make a mistake. But, don't worry; that happens to everyone. As you sign more, you will get better and your confidence will grow. In a short time, you'll surprise yourself and even your friends. I know you can do it. Have fun with *Signing for Kids*.

Did You Know?

- More than 28 million people in the United States have a hearing loss of some degree.
- American Sign Language was created by deaf people in the United States to communicate with each other. It's their natural language.
- Approximately 90 percent of deaf children are born to hearing parents.
- Thomas Hopkins Gallaudet founded the first school for deaf people in the United States in 1817, in Hartford, Connecticut.
- The only liberal arts college for deaf people in the world is Gallaudet College, which was founded in Washington, D.C., in 1864.
- American Sign Language is one of the most commonly used languages in the United States.

Basic Hand Shapes

Become familiar with these basic hand shapes. They are used in many of the descriptions to help form the signs correctly.

Closed Hand
The hand is closed in the shape of an *S* hand.

Curved Hand
The fingers are curved and touching. Sometimes "curved *open* hand" is used, where the fingers are kept bent but spread apart.

Open Hand
The hand is held flat, fingers apart. Sometimes called a "flat *open* hand."

Flat Hand
The hand is held flat with fingers touching.

The *And* Hand
When the "*and* hand" is mentioned only the ending position is being referred to with all fingertips touching.

Bent Hand
The fingers are touching and bent at the knuckles.

Clawed Hand
The fingers are held apart and bent.

Manual Alphabet

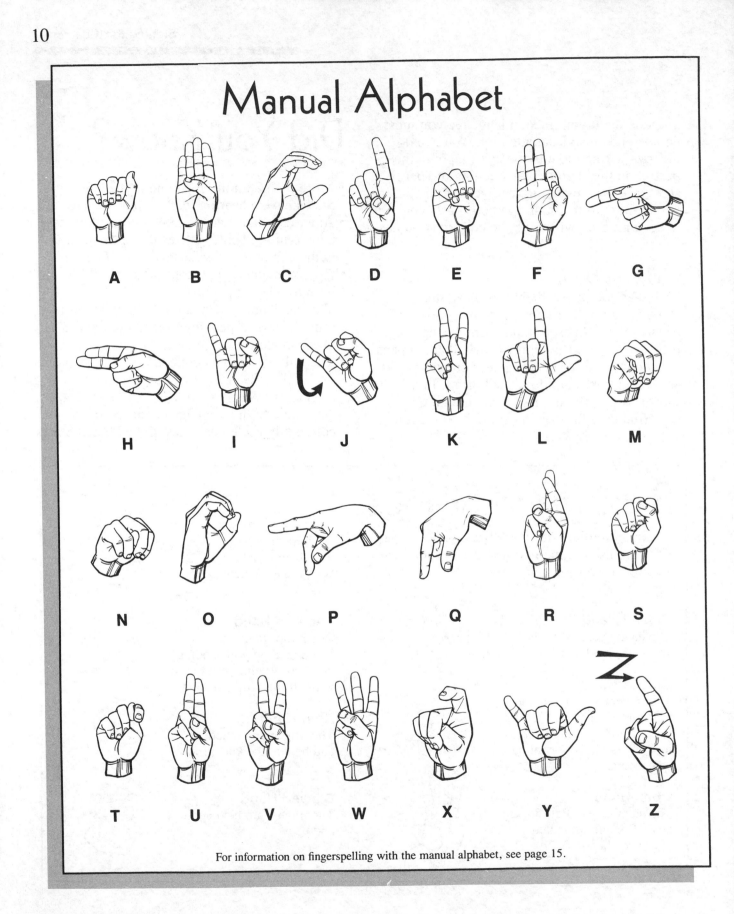

For information on fingerspelling with the manual alphabet, see page 15.

PETS & ANIMALS 1

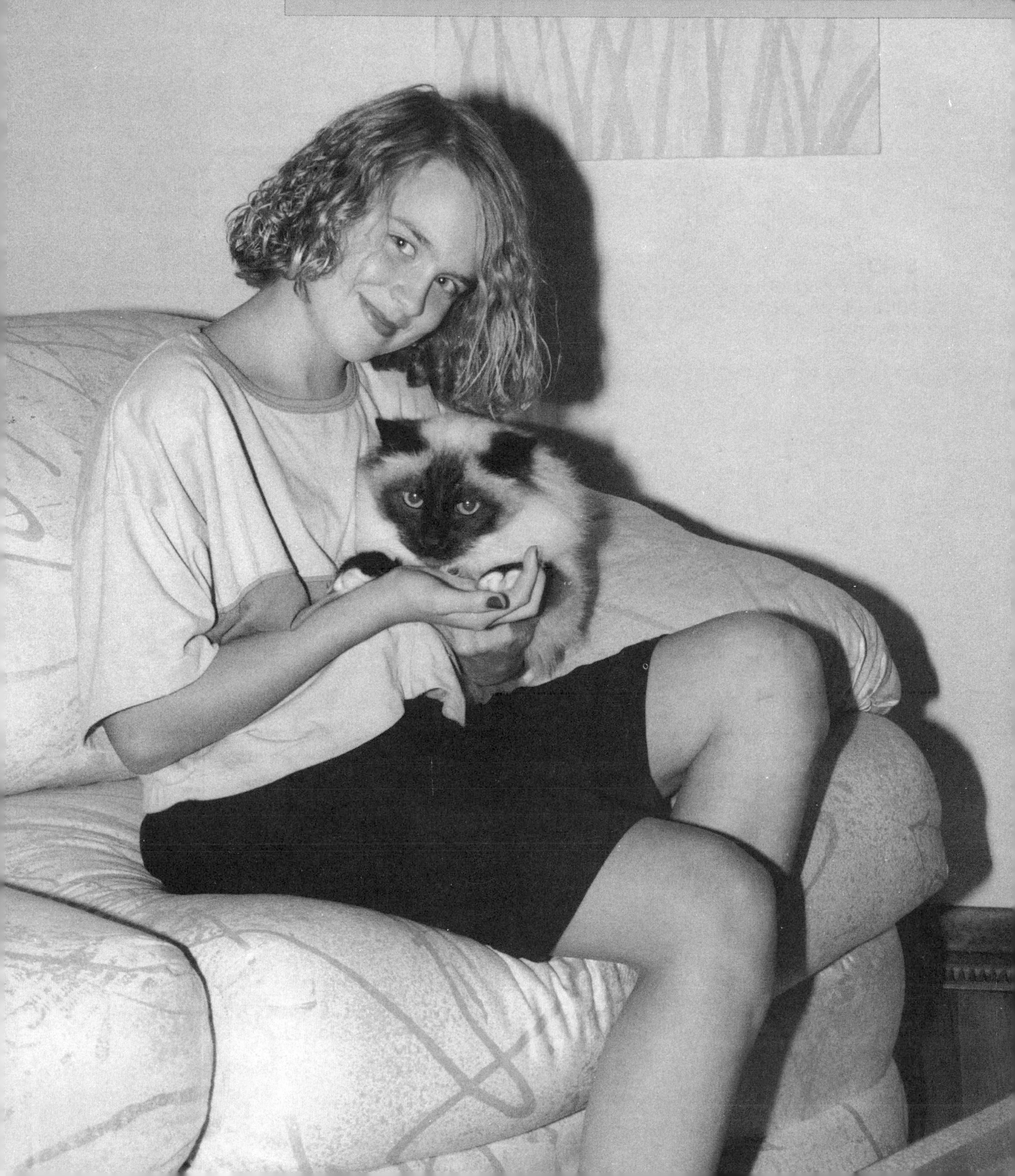

BIRD

Place the right Q hand at the right side of the mouth, with the fingers pointing forward. Close and open the Q fingers a few times.

CAT

Place the index fingers and thumbs of the F hands under the nose, with the palms facing each other; then move the hands out sideways. This sign may also be done with the right hand only.

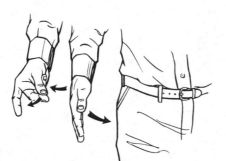

DOG

Slap the right flat hand against the right leg, and then snap the right middle finger.

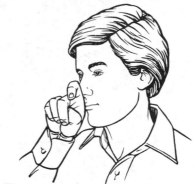

EAGLE

Place the right X hand in front of the nose, with the palm facing forward.

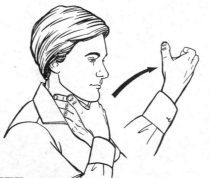

GIRAFFE

Place the thumb and index finger of the left C hand on the neck. Touch the neck with the thumb and index finger of the right C hand, and then move the right hand in a forward-upward direction.

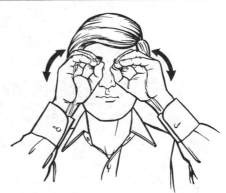

OWL

Look through both O hands and twist them toward the center and back a few times.

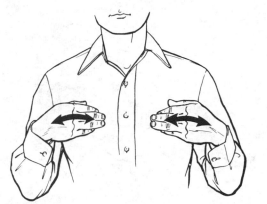

ANIMAL

Place the fingertips of both bent hands on the chest. Maintain the position of the fingertips while rocking both hands in and out sideways.

BEAR

Cross the arms in front of the chest, with the palms facing the body. Make a few downward and inward clawing movements with both hands.

COW

Place the thumb tips of both *Y* hands against the temples and twist the hands upward so that the little fingers point up (sometimes the action is reversed). This sign is often done with the right hand only.

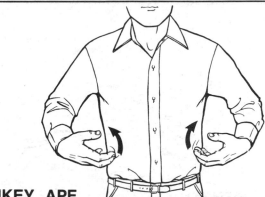

MONKEY, APE

Scratch the sides of the chest with both claw-shaped hands.

PIG, HOG

Place the back of the right flat hand under the chin, with the fingers pointing to the left. Bend and unbend the hand several times at the knuckles.

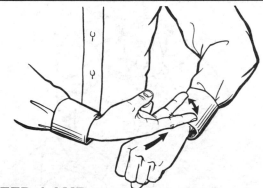

SHEEP, LAMB

Place the back of the right *V* fingers on the left arm, with the palm facing down. Open and close the *V* fingers as they move up the arm. To sign *lamb*, add the sign for *small* (page 96).

DEER, ANTLERS, MOOSE

With the palms facing forward, touch the temples with the thumbs of both open hands a few times. *Moose* can be signed with the same movement but with the fingers closed rather than open.

ELEPHANT

Place the back of the right curved hand in front of the mouth. Move the right hand down and then forward and upward. Let the fingertips lead the way throughout the movement.

FISH (noun)

Place the fingertips of the left flat hand at the right wrist or elbow. Point the right flat hand forward with the palm facing left, and swing it from right to left a few times. Most of the movement is at the wrist.

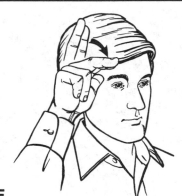

HORSE

Extend the thumb of the right *U* hand and place it on the right temple, with the palm facing forward. Bend and unbend the *U* fingers a few times.

SKUNK

Point the right *K* fingers down in front of the forehead, with the palm facing the head. Move the right hand backward over the top of the head.

TIGER

Place the fingers of both slightly curved open hands in front of the face, with the palms facing in. Pull the hands apart sideways while changing to claw-shaped hands. Repeat a few times.

Fingerspelling & Name Signs

Fingerspelling is used to spell out words one letter at a time with the manual alphabet. It is used for names of people, places, and words for which there are no signs, or as a substitute when the sign has not been learned. When fingerspelling, hold your hand in a comfortable position near the right shoulder, palm facing forward. Be careful not to block your mouth from view. Combine letters smoothly and clearly to form words. Say the word as you begin to spell it, but not individual letters. Pause, for just a moment, after the last letter in each word. Don't make exaggerated hand or arm movements. Begin to fingerspell by practicing two- and three-letter words; then move on to larger words. Try to develop a rhythm as you fingerspell, and don't worry about speed. It will come with practice.

Fingerspelling Position

If a word has double letters (for instance, *keep*), open the hand slightly between the signs for those letters. When the hand is already open (as for *C* and *L*), move the hand to the right with a small bounce for the second open letter.

When someone is fingerspelling to you, try to read the words in syllables, not the individual letters. It is helpful to have a friend to practice with, but when you don't, why not try fingerspelling in front of a mirror?

Name Signs

Name signs are shortcuts to fingerspelling a person's name. Since fingerspelling is slower, it's good to have a name sign. To develop one, think of an outstanding quality you have and use your first initial. Here's an example: Trisha has long black hair. So, her name sign could be a *T* hand touching the hair or going down the right side of the head. Always fingerspell your name first, especially when meeting deaf people. Then use your name sign. Try making up one for yourself. Or you can use your full initials instead.

Fingerspelling Fun

Once you know the manual alphabet, practice fingerspelling the following groups of letters until you feel comfortable. Then try longer words.

ad	bad	bag	ham	bay	get	big	bit	dip	bear	bake	fill	fine
Al	dad	lag	jam	day	jet	dig	fit	hip	dear	cake	hill	line
am	had	nag	Pam	hay	let	pig	hit	lip	fear	Jake	pill	mine
an	mad	rag	ram	may	net	rig	nit	rip	hear	lake	sill	nine
as	sad	sag	Sam	pay	set	wig	pit	tip	near	make	till	pine
at	tad	tag	yam	say	wet	zig	sit	zip	year	take	will	vine

CHICKEN

Open and close the right index finger and thumb in front of the mouth. Sometimes these fingers are also brought down into the upturned left palm with a pecking motion.

GOAT

Place the thumb side of the right *S* hand on the point of the chin. Move the right hand up to the forehead while changing to a *V* hand, with the palm facing left.

KANGAROO

Hold the right bent hand to the front, with the palm facing forward. Move the hand forward with several up-and-down movements.

MOUSE

Brush the right index finger to the left across the tip of the nose a few times.

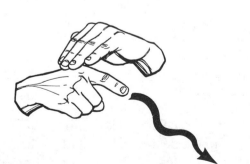

SNAKE

Move the right index finger forward in small spiral circles as it passes under the downturned palm of the left flat hand.

TURKEY

With the palm facing down, shake the right *Q* fingers back and forth in front of the chin; then move the *Q* hand forward and down with a few small spirals.

DUCK

Point the right *N* fingers and thumb forward in front of the mouth. Open and close the *N* fingers and thumb a few times.

FOX

Place the circle formed by the thumb and index finger of the right *F* hand over the nose, with the palm facing left. Twist the hand so that the palm faces down.

RABBIT

Cross the *H* hands at the wrists, with the palms facing the body. Bend and unbend the *H* fingers a few times.

SQUIRREL, CHIPMUNK

Hold the curved fingers of both *V* hands to the front, with the palms facing each other. Tap the fingertips of both *V* hands against each other a few times.

TURTLE

Place the right *A* hand under the palm-down left curved hand. Expose the right thumb from under the little-finger edge of the left hand and wiggle it up and down.

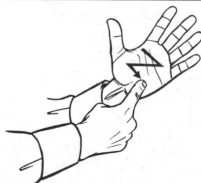

ZOO

Hold up the left flat open hand, with the palm facing forward. Trace the letter *Z* across the front of the left hand with the right index finger. This sign is often fingerspelled.

The Animal Connection

Draw a line connecting each sign with the correct word at the left or right side of the box. Answers are at bottom of page.

SNACKS & FOOD 2

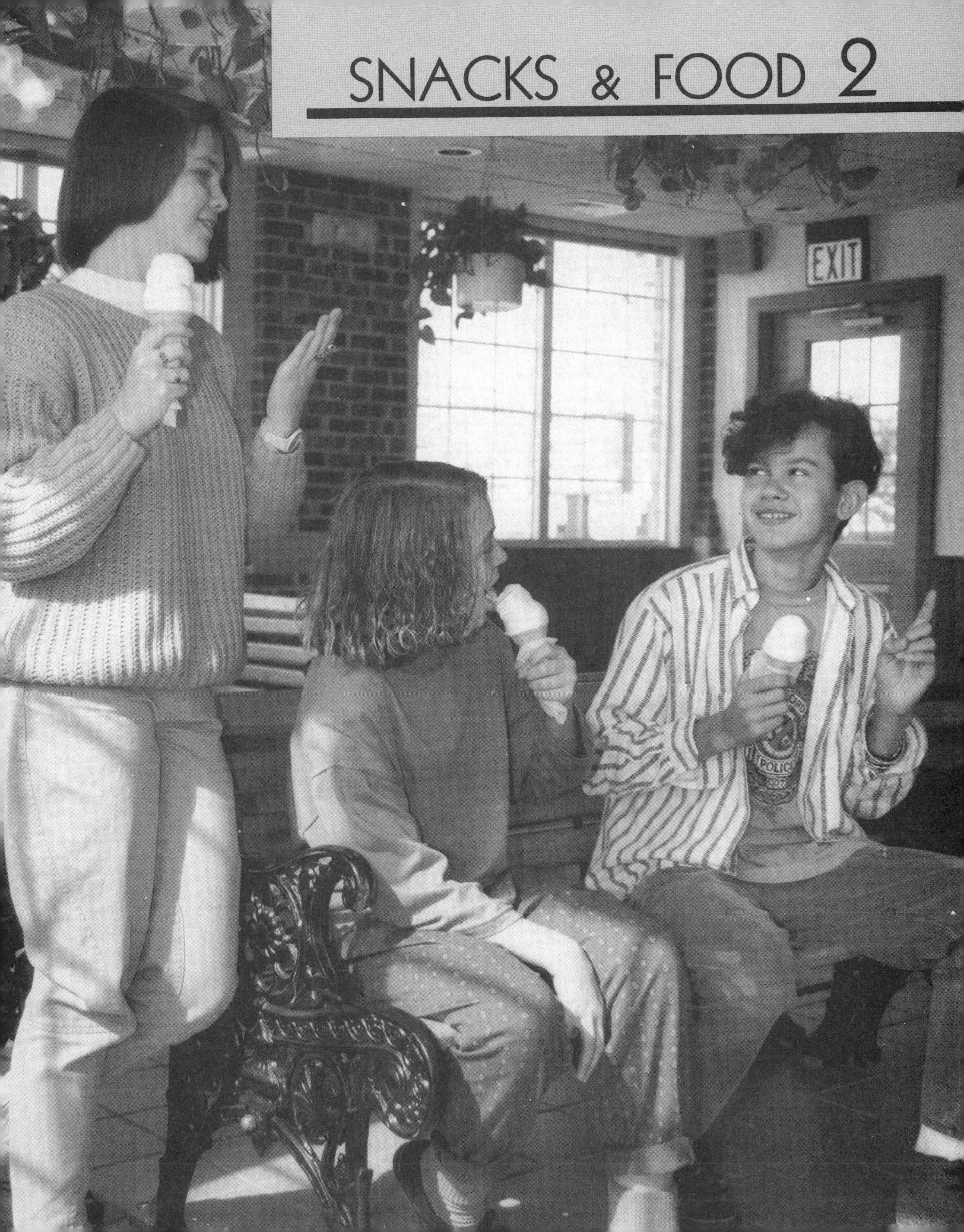

CANDY
Brush the tips of the right *U* fingers downward over the lips and chin a few times.

CHOCOLATE
Make a few small counterclockwise circles with the thumb of the right *C* hand over the back of the left flat hand.

COOKIE
Place the right *C* thumb and fingertips into the left flat palm and twist. Repeat a few times.

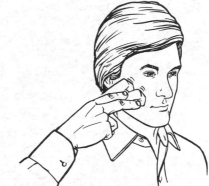

GUM (chewing)
Place the right *V* fingertips on the right cheek. Bend and straighten the *V* fingers a few times as the fingertips remain on the cheek.

ICE CREAM
Pull the right *S* hand toward the mouth with a downward twist a few times. The tongue may also be shown.

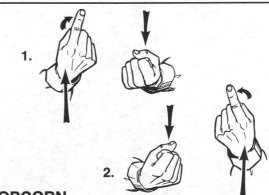

POPCORN
Hold both *S* hands in front with the palms facing up. Flick both index fingers up alternately several times.

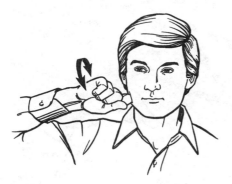

APPLE
Twist the knuckle of the index finger of the right closed hand back and forth on the right cheek.

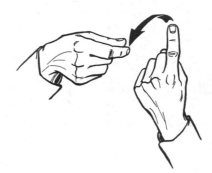

BANANA
Hold up the left index finger, with the palm facing in; then with the right hand make the natural movement of peeling a banana.

CAKE
Move the fingertips and thumb of the right C hand forward across the left flat hand from wrist to fingertips.

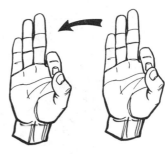

FRENCH FRIES
Sign the right F hand once, then a second time slightly to the right.

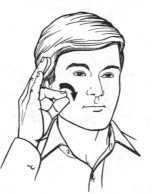

FRUIT
Place the thumb and index finger of the right F hand on the right cheek. Twist the hand forward or backward.

HAMBURGER
Cup the right hand on top of the left cupped hand; then reverse.

CHEESE

Place the heels of both hands together and rotate them back and forth in opposite directions.

PIZZA

Outline the shape of a Z in front of the chest with the P hand.

RESTAURANT

With the palm facing left, move the fingers of the right R hand from the right to the left of the mouth.

SANDWICH

Place the fingertips of both palm-to-palm hands near the mouth.

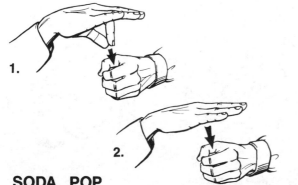

SODA, POP

Put the thumb and index finger of the right F hand into the left O hand. Then open the right hand and slap the left O hand with it.

SPAGHETTI

Touch the fingertips of both I hands to each other; then make small spirals with the little fingers while drawing both hands apart to the sides.

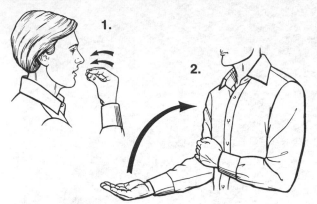

BREAKFAST

Move the fingers of the right closed *and* hand to the mouth a few times. Place the left flat hand into the bend of the right elbow; then raise the right forearm upward.

COOK (verb or noun), FRY

Place first the palm side and then the back of the right flat hand on the upturned palm of the left flat hand.

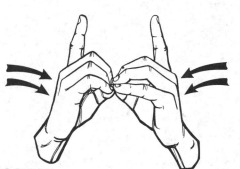

DESSERT

Bring the thumbs of both upright *D* hands together a few times.

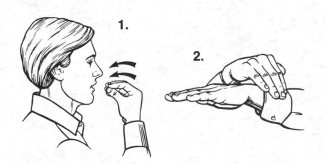

DINNER, SUPPER

Move the fingers of the right closed *and* hand to the mouth a few times, and then place the right curved hand over the back of the left flat hand.

EAT, FOOD

Move the right *and* hand toward the mouth a few times.

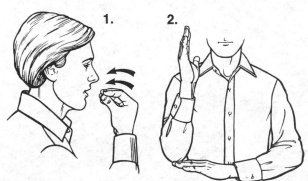

LUNCH

Move the fingers of the right closed *and* hand to the mouth a few times. Place the left flat hand at the outer bend of the right elbow, and raise the right forearm to an upright position with the palm facing left.

BREAD

Draw the little-finger edge of the right hand down a few times over the back of the left flat hand, which has its palm facing the body.

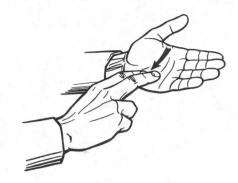

BUTTER

Quickly brush the fingertips of the right *H* hand across the left palm a few times.

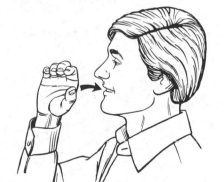

DRINK

Move the right *C* hand in a short arc toward the mouth.

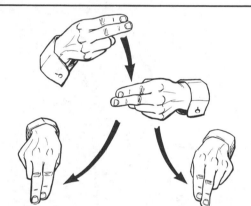

EGG

Bring the middle finger of the right *H* hand down on the index finger of the left *H* hand, and move both hands down and out. Most of the latter movement can be done from the wrists.

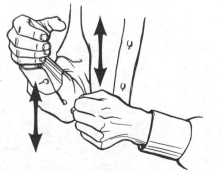

MILK

Squeeze one or both slightly open *S* hands with a downward motion. Do it alternately if two hands are used.

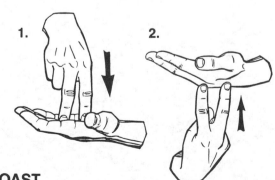

TOAST

Move the fingers of the right *V* hand down onto the left palm, then up against the back of the left flat hand.

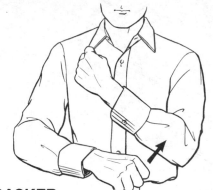

CRACKER
Strike the right *S* hand near the left elbow.

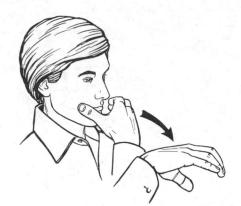

HOT
Place the fingers and thumb of the right *C* hand at the sides of the mouth; then quickly twist the hand forward to the right.

HUNGRY
Move the thumb and fingers of the right *C* hand down the center of the chest from just below the throat.

JELLY
Rub the tip of the little finger of the right *J* hand across the left palm once or twice.

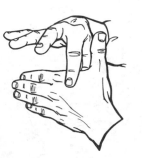

MEAT
Pinch the flesh of the left flat hand with the right thumb and index finger.

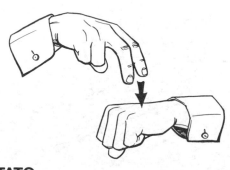

POTATO
Strike the fingertips of the right curved *V* hand on the back of the left downturned *S* hand.

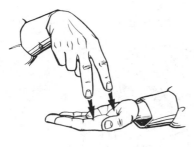

FORK

Move the fingers of the right *V* hand onto the left upturned palm a few times.

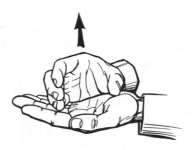

GLASS (drinking)

Place the little-finger edge of the right *C* hand on the left flat palm and raise the right hand a short distance.

KNIFE

Move the fingers (or just the index) of the right *H* hand downward across the fingers (or just the index) of the left *H* hand several times.

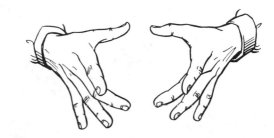

PLATE

Make a circle with the thumbs and fingers of both hands.

SPOON

Lift the fingers of the right curved *H* hand up from the palm of the left slightly curved hand toward the mouth a few times.

WATER

Touch the mouth with the index finger of the right *W* hand a few times.

Guess the Snack

Draw a line connecting each sign to the
corresponding word in the center of the page.
Answers are at bottom of page.

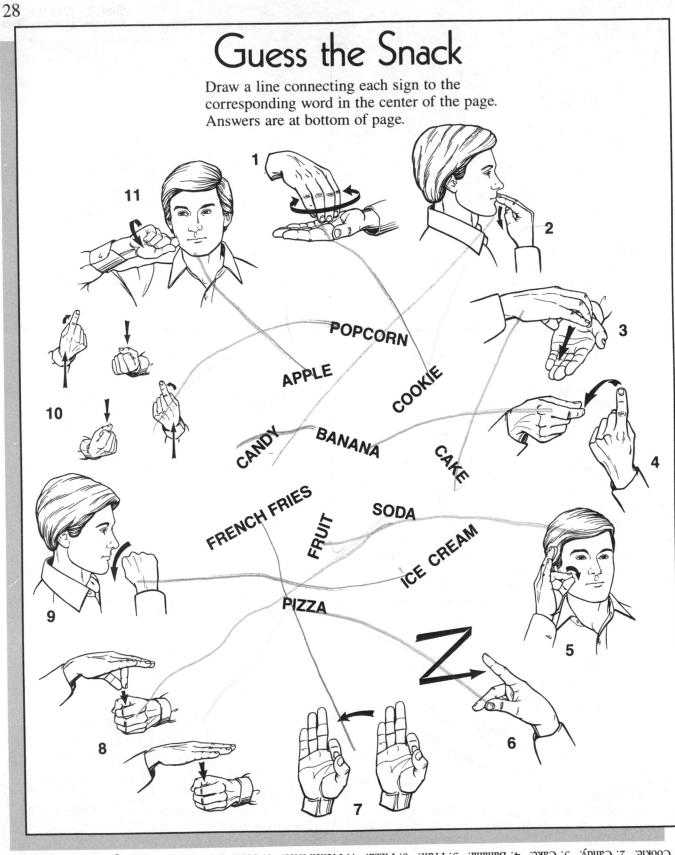

POPCORN

APPLE

COOKIE

CANDY

BANANA

CAKE

FRENCH FRIES

FRUIT

SODA

ICE CREAM

PIZZA

FAMILY, FRIENDS & PEOPLE 3

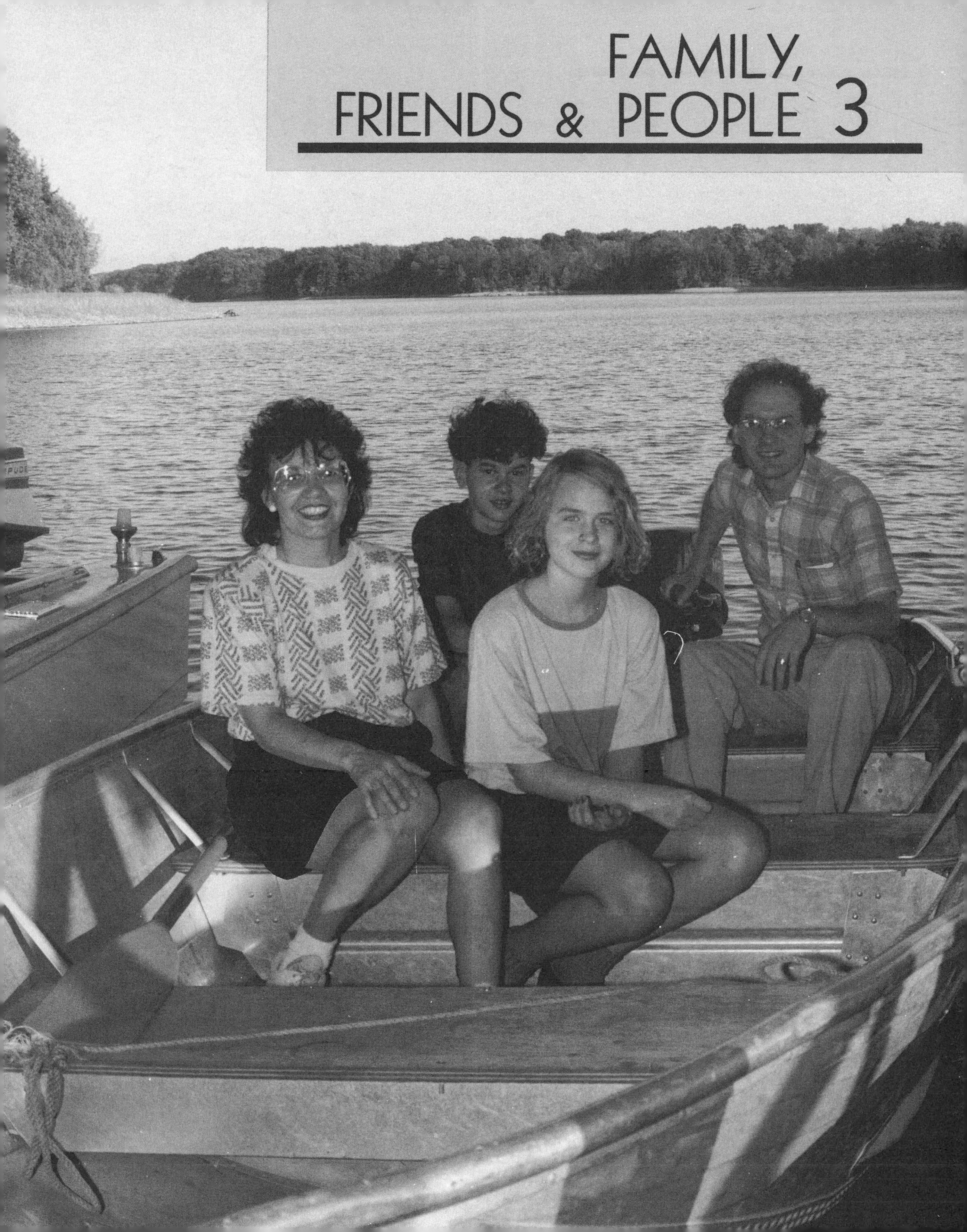

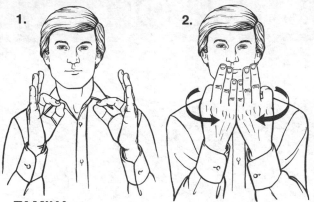

FAMILY

Place both upright *F* hands to the front with the palms facing each other. Make an outward circular movement with each hand at the same time until the little fingers touch.

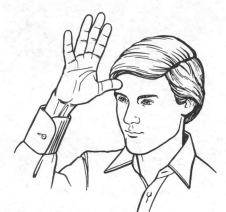

FATHER

The informal but commonly used sign is made by touching the forehead with the thumb of the right open hand. The fingers may be wiggled slightly.

MOTHER

The informal but commonly used sign is made by touching the right chin or cheek with the thumb of the right open hand. The fingers may be wiggled slightly.

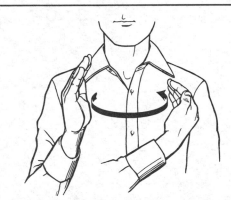

OUR

Place the slightly cupped right hand on the right side of the chest, with the palm facing left. Move the right hand forward in a circular motion, and bring it to rest near the left shoulder, with the palm facing right.

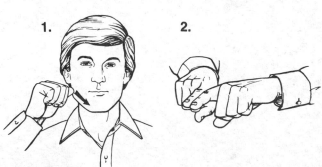

SISTER

Trace the right side of the jaw from ear to chin with the palm side of the right *A*-hand thumb. Then, with one movement, point both index fingers forward and bring them together.

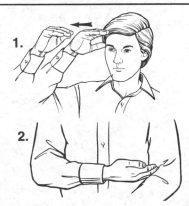

SON

Move the right hand to the forehead as if gripping the bill of a cap. Then move the right flat hand, with the palm facing up, into the crook of the left bent elbow.

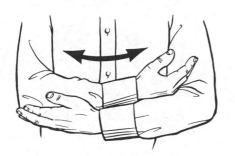

BABY
Hold the arms in the natural position for cradling a baby and rock the arms sideways.

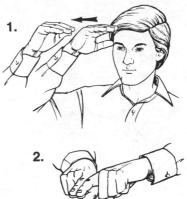

BROTHER
Move the right hand to the forehead as if gripping the bill of a cap. Then, with one movement, point both index fingers forward and bring them together.

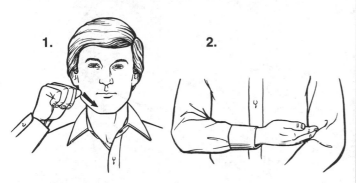

DAUGHTER
Trace the right side of the jaw from ear to chin with the palm side of the right A-hand thumb. Then move the right flat hand, with the palm facing up, into the crook of the left bent elbow.

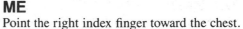

ME
Point the right index finger toward the chest.

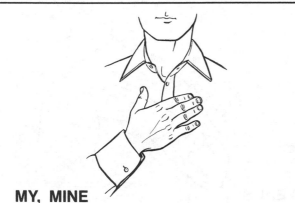

MY, MINE
Place the palm of the right flat hand on the chest.

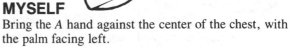

MYSELF
Bring the A hand against the center of the chest, with the palm facing left.

AUNT
Place the right *A* hand close to the right cheek and shake the hand back and forth from the wrist.

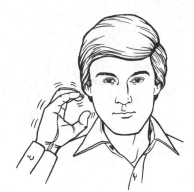

COUSIN
Place the right *C* hand close to the right temple (for a male cousin) or close to the right cheek (for a female); then shake the hand back and forth from the wrist.

GRANDFATHER
Touch the forehead with the thumb of the right open hand, with the palm facing left. Move the right hand in two forward arcs.

GRANDMOTHER
Touch the chin with the thumb of the right open hand, with the palm facing left. Move the right hand in two forward arcs.

UNCLE
With the palm facing forward, place the right *U* hand close to the right temple and shake it back and forth from the wrist.

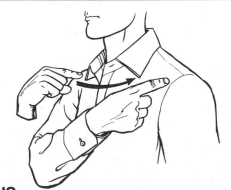

WE, US
Touch the right shoulder with the right index finger; then move the finger in a forward semicircle until it touches the left shoulder.

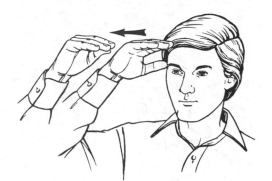

BOY, MALE
Move the right hand to the forehead as if gripping the bill of a cap.

CUTE
Stroke the chin several times with the fingers of the right *U* hand.

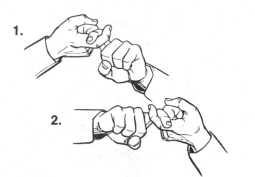

FRIEND
Interlock the right and left index fingers and repeat in reverse.

GIRL, FEMALE
Trace the right side of the jaw from ear to chin with the palm side of the right *A*-hand thumb.

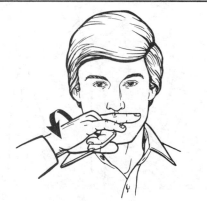

KID
Extend the index and the little finger of the right hand. With the palm facing down, put the index finger under the nose. Then move the hand up and down slightly.

NAME
Cross the middle-finger edge of the right *H* fingers over the index-finger edge of the left *H* fingers.

HIS, HER (possessive)

Push the right flat hand forward with the palm facing out and slightly in the direction of the person being referred to.

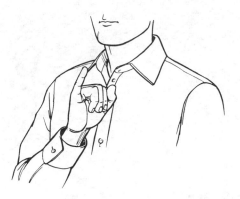

I

Position the right *I* hand with the palm facing left and the thumb touching the chest.

I LOVE YOU

Hold up the right hand with the palm facing forward and the thumb, index, and little finger extended.

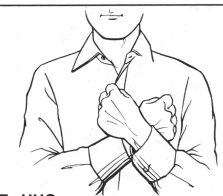

LOVE, HUG

Cross both closed or flat hands over the heart, with the palms facing in.

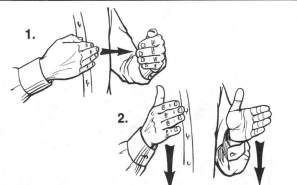

NEIGHBOR

Hold the left curved hand away from the body, with the palm facing in. Move the back of the right curved hand close to the palm of the left. Then bring both flat hands down with the palms facing each other.

YOU

Point the right index finger to the person being addressed. If referring to several people, make a sweeping motion from left to right.

FAMOUS
Point both index fingers toward the mouth and move them outward and upward in small circles.

PEOPLE
Make inward circles alternately from the sides with both *P* hands.

PERSON
Place both *P* hands forward; then move them down at the same time.

PERSON ENDING
Hold both flat open hands to the front with the palms facing each other; then move both hands down at the same time.

WEDDING
Point the fingers of both flat hands down from the wrists in the front. Swing the hands toward each other until the left fingers and thumb grasp the right fingers.

WHO
Make a counterclockwise circle in front of the lips with the right index finger.

DIVORCE
Hold both *D* hands with palms facing and fingertips touching. Twist both hands outward and sideways until the palms face forward.

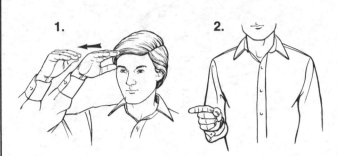

HE, HIM
Move the right hand to the forehead as if gripping the bill of a cap. Then point the index finger forward. If it is obvious that a male is being referred to, the sign for *male* (the first movement) may be omitted.

MAN
Touch the thumb of the right open hand to the forehead, then to the chest.

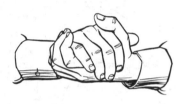

MARRY
Clasp the hands in a natural position with the right hand above the left.

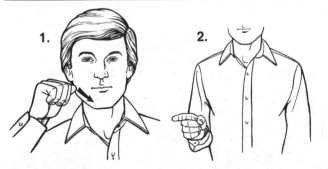

SHE, HER
Trace the right side of the jaw from ear to chin with the palm side of the right *A*-hand thumb. Then point the index finger forward. If it is obvious that a female is being referred to, the sign for *female* (the first movement) may be omitted.

WOMAN
Touch the thumb of the right open hand to the chin, then to the chest.

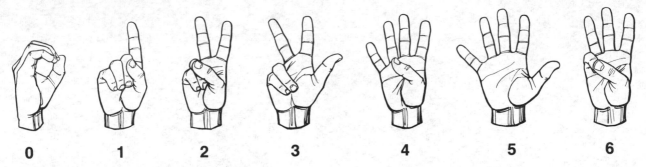

0 **1** **2** **3** **4** **5** **6**

The right palm faces forward, unless indicated otherwise
by the illustration or description.

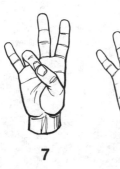  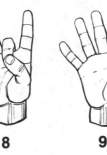

7 **8** **9**

10 Shake the *A* hand.

11 Flick the right index finger
up with the palm facing the body.

12 Flick the right index and
middle finger up with the palm
facing the body.

13 Move the fingers of the
right *3* hand up and down
with the palm facing the body.

14 Move the fingers of the
right *4* hand up and down
with the palm facing the body.

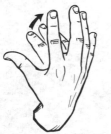

15 Move the fingers of the
right *5* hand up and down
with the palm facing the body.

16 Sign *10*, then *6*.

17 Sign *10*, then *7*.

   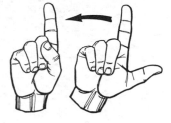

18 Sign *10*, then *8*.   **19** Sign *10*, then *9*.   **20**   **21**

 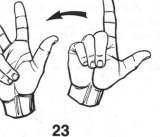 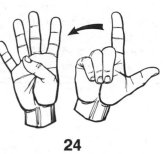

22   **23**   **24**

  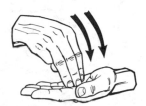

ONE HUNDRED
Sign *1*, then *C*.

THOUSAND Bring the fingertips of the right *M* hand down onto the left flat hand.

MILLION Bring the fingertips of the right *M* hand down onto the left flat palm twice.

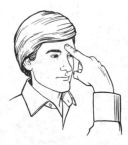

CENTS
Touch the forehead with the right extended index finger and sign the desired number.

EIGHT CENTS
Touch the forehead with the right extended index finger and move it forward while twisting the wrist to sign *8*. This number is signed by touching the middle finger to the thumb, with the other fingers pointing up and separated and the palm forward.

Money amounts, years, addresses and telephone numbers are signed as they are spoken in English. To express the amount $16.24, sign *16 dollars 24 cents*. For the year 1976, sign *19 7 6* (not *70 6*). The address 348 River Road is signed *3 4 8 River Road* (the words are fingerspelled). The digits of a telephone number are signed as they are spoken; the number 555-4844, for example, is signed *5 5 5 4 8 4 4*.

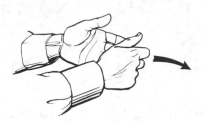

DOLLARS

Point the fingers of the left flat hand to the right. Grasp the fingers between the right palm and fingers (or thumb and fingers); then pull the right hand away from the left a few times.

 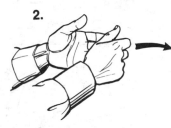

NINE DOLLARS

Sign *9* by touching the right index finger to the thumb, with the other fingers pointing straight up. Then sign *dollars*.

MONEY

Strike the back of the right *and* hand on the left upturned palm a few times.

OWE

Tap the left palm with the right index finger several times.

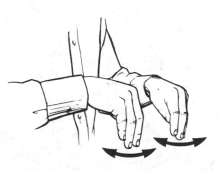

STORE, SELL

Point both *and* hands down with bent wrists, and twist them in and out from the body a few times.

BORROW

Cross the *V* hands at the wrists (the sign for *keep*) and move them toward the body.

BUY

Move the back of the right *and* hand down into the upturned palm of the left hand, then up and straight out or slightly to the right.

CHEAP

Hold the left flat hand with the fingers pointing forward and the palm facing right. Brush the index-finger side of the slightly curved right hand downward across the palm of the left hand.

COLLECT, EARN

Move the little-finger edge of the right curved hand across the left upturned flat hand from fingertips to wrist. End with the right hand closed.

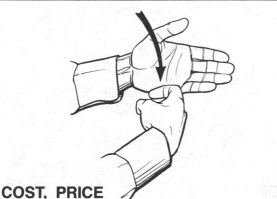

COST, PRICE

Strike the right crooked index finger against the left flat palm with a downward movement.

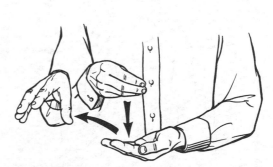

EXPENSIVE

Strike the back of the right *and* hand on the left upturned palm; then lift the right hand and open it while moving it to the right.

ALL, WHOLE
Hold the left flat hand to the front with the palm facing the body. Move the right flat hand, with the palm facing out, over-down-in-up, and end with the back of the right hand in the palm of the left hand.

FULL, FILLED
Move the right flat open hand to the left, over the thumb edge of the left closed hand.

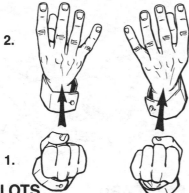

MANY, LOTS
Hold both *S* hands to the front with the palms facing up. Flick the fingers and thumbs open several times.

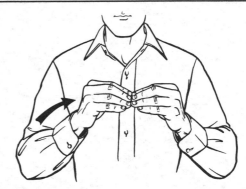

MORE
Touch the fingertips of both *and* hands in front of the chest, with the palms facing down. The right hand can be brought up to meet the left from a slightly lower position.

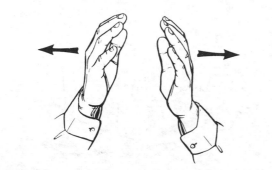

MUCH, A LOT
Place both slightly curved open hands to the front with the palms facing; then draw them apart to the sides.

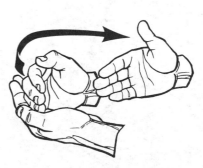

SOME
Place the little-finger edge of the slightly curved right hand on the left flat palm. Pull the right hand toward the body while forming a flat right hand.

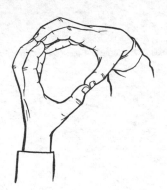

BALL, ROUND
Curve both hands with the fingertips touching, as if holding a ball. Thumbs and index fingers should face the observer.

BASEBALL
Place the right *S* hand above the left *S* hand and swing them forward together from the right of the body to the center.

CLUB, TEAM
Hold both *C* hands upright in front of the chest, with the palms facing. Move the hands outward in a circle until the little fingers touch. For *team*, use *T* hands.

PRACTICE
Rub the knuckles of the right *A* hand back and forth across the left index finger.

THROW
Place the right *A* hand beside the right side of the head. Move the right hand quickly forward and open it at the same time.

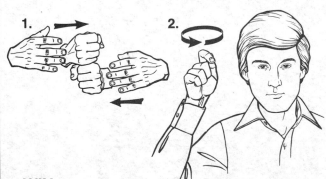

WIN
Bring both open hands together while forming *S* hands, and place the right hand on top of the left. Hold up either one or both closed hands with the tips of the thumb and index finger touching.

BASKETBALL
Hold both curved open hands at head level and move them forward and upward.

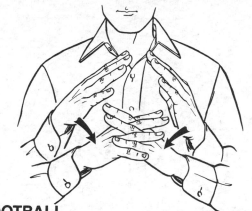

FOOTBALL
Interlock the fingers of both hands vigorously a few times.

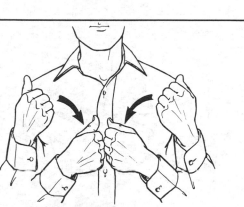

GAME, CHALLENGE
Hold both *A* hands in front and to the sides of the chest, with the palms facing the body. Bring the hands firmly together until the knuckles touch.

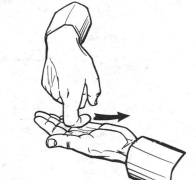

HOCKEY
Brush the knuckles of the right *X* finger across the left flat palm a few times.

ICE SKATING
Hold both *X* hands to the front with the palms facing up. Move the hands alternately forward and backward.

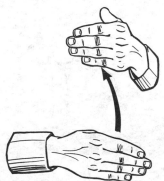

SOCCER, KICK
Sweep the flat index side of the right hand upward to strike the little-finger edge of the flat or closed left hand.

BICYCLE
Move both downturned *S* hands forward in alternate circles.

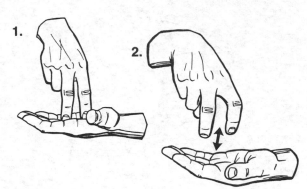

JUMP
Imitate a jumping motion with the fingers of the right *V* hand on the left flat palm.

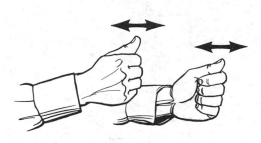

RACE
Hold both *A* hands to the front with the palms facing. Move the hands quickly back and forth alternately.

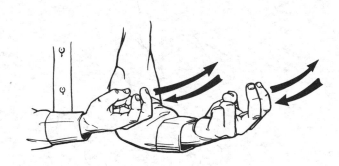

ROLLER SKATING
Hold both curved *V* fingers to the front with the palms facing up. Move the hands alternately forward and backward.

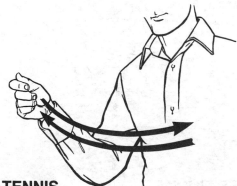

TENNIS
Extend the right arm to the right with the hand closed. Move the arm forward across to the left and back to the right.

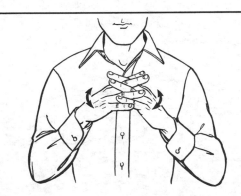

WRESTLING
Interlock the fingers of both hands and move them back and forth in front of the chest.

SKATEBOARDING, SKATEBOARD

Place the right *H* fingers on top of left *H* fingers and move hands ahead together in a wavy motion.

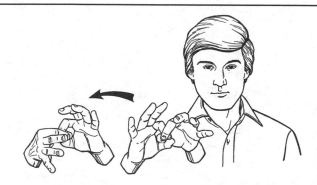

OLYMPICS

Form *F* hands and interlock the thumbs and index fingers a few times as the hands move to the right.

JOGGING

Place both partially open *A* hands to the front with palms facing. Move them back and forth alternately.

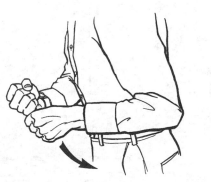

CANOEING

Hold the right *S* hand over the left *S* hand at the left (or right) of the body. Move them together down and backward.

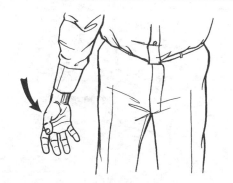

BOWLING

Swing the right curved hand forward from behind the body to the front.

ART, DRAW
Trace a wavy line over the left flat palm with the right *I* finger.

DRUMS
Imitate the movement of playing drums with the two *A* hands.

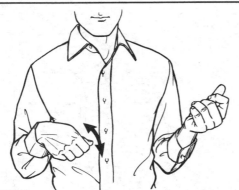

GUITAR
Pretend to be holding a guitar with the left hand while strumming the front of the guitar with the right *A* hand.

 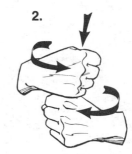

MAKE
Strike the right *S* hand on top of the left *S* hand and twist the hands slightly inward. Repeat for emphasis as needed.

MUSIC, SING, SONG
Wave the right flat hand from left to right in front of the left flat hand, which has its palm facing right.

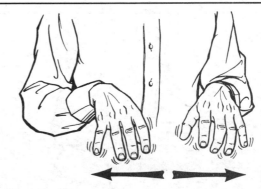

PIANO
Hold both downturned curved open hands to the front; then move them to the left and right while making downward striking movements with the fingers.

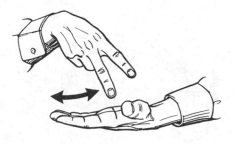

DANCE

Point the left flat upturned hand to the right; then swing the downturned fingers of the right *V* hand from side to side over the left palm.

FIREWORKS

With the palms facing forward, open and close both *S* hands alternately with upward movements.

FUN

Brush the tip of the nose with the fingers of the right *U* hand. Move the hand down, and brush the left and right *U* fingers up and down against each other a few times.

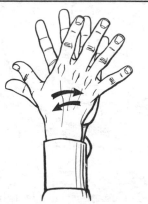

MOVIE

Place both flat open hands palm to palm, with the left palm facing somewhat forward. Slide the right hand back and forth over the left hand a few times. Most of the movement is from the right wrist.

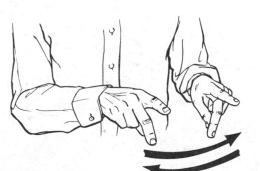

PARTY

Hold both *P* hands in front and swing them back and forth from left to right.

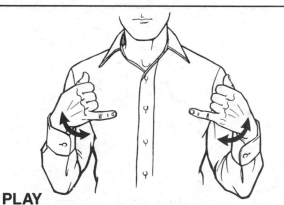

PLAY

Hold both *Y* hands in front of the chest and twist them up and down a few times.

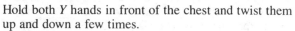

CLIMB

With the palms of both curved *V* hands facing each other, make a climbing motion with each hand alternately.

GOLF

Point the right *A* hand down at waist level with the thumb side of the left *A* hand touching the little-finger side of the right hand. Swing both hands from right to left.

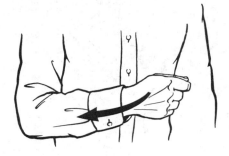

PING-PONG

Go through the natural movement of swinging a Ping-Pong paddle back and forth with the right hand. Most of the movement is from the wrist.

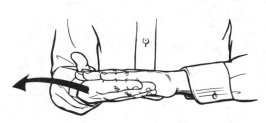

RUN

Place both flat hands palm to palm, with the right hand under the left. Slide the right hand quickly forward.

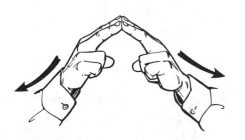

TENT, CAMP

Form the point of a triangle with the fingers of both *V* hands, then separate the hands by moving them down and to the sides a short distance. *Camp* is signed by repeating the sign a few times, with the hands moved to the right.

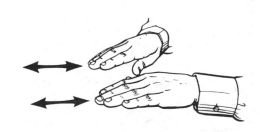

WALK

Hold both flat hands in front with the palms down; then imitate walking by moving each hand forward alternately.

ARCHERY

Stretch the left *S* hand out sideways; then bring the right curved *V* fingers back from behind the left hand to a closed-hand position just under the chin.

FISHING

Position the left hand above the right as if holding a fishing rod. Move the hands quickly up and back from the wrist.

PLAYING CARDS

Pretend you are holding a deck of cards in the left *A* hand. Hold the right *A* hand close to the left and move it forward, changing it to a *3* hand as if dealing out cards.

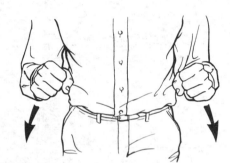

SKIING

Hold both *S* hands in front and to the sides. Push down and back with both hands at the same time.

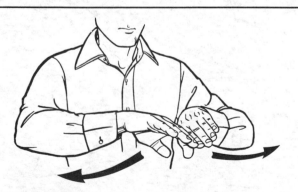

SWIMMING

Place both slightly curved hands to the front with the backs of the hands partially facing each other and the fingers pointing forward. Move the hands forward and to the sides at the same time.

VOLLEYBALL

Hold both flat hands at head level, with the palms facing forward. Move the hands forward and upward.

Find the Sport Signs

How many sport signs can you find? Circle the number next to each one. Answers are at bottom of page.

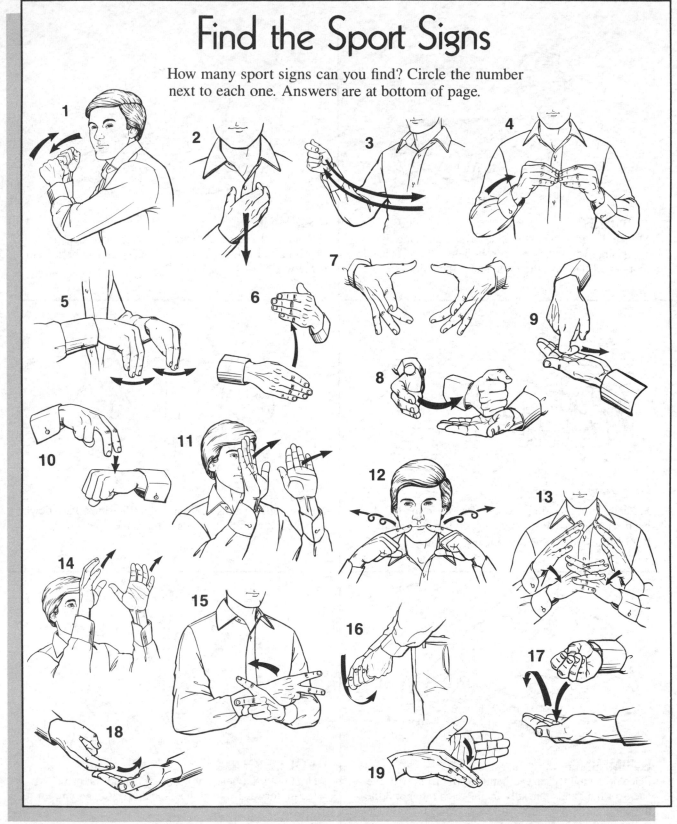

AFTERNOON

Hold the left arm horizontal, pointing to the right. The left hand is flat with the palm facing down. Place the right forearm on the back of the left hand at a 45-degree angle.

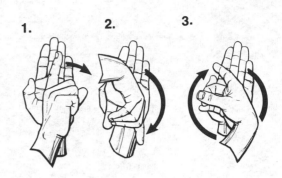

HOUR

Point the fingers of the left flat hand up with the palm facing right. Move the index finger of the right *D* hand in a clockwise circle by turning the wrist. Keep the right index finger in constant contact with the left hand.

MINUTE, SECOND

Hold the left flat hand vertical with the palm facing right. Touch the left palm with the index finger of the right *D* hand. The index points up. For *minute*, move the index finger past the little finger of the left hand. For *second*, move the index finger to the little finger.

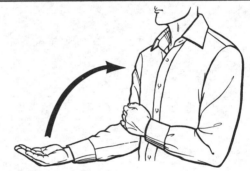

MORNING

Place the left flat hand, with the palm facing the body, in the bend of the right elbow. Bring the right flat hand toward the body until the arm is upright, with the palm facing the body.

NIGHT

Hold the left arm horizontal, with the fingers of the left downturned flat hand pointing right. Place the right forearm on the back of the left hand and point the right curved hand downward.

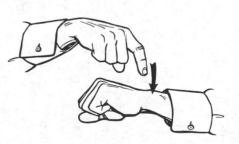

TIME

Tap the tip of the right curved index finger on the back of the left wrist a few times.

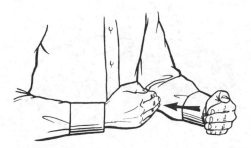

BEFORE (time)
Hold the left slightly curved hand out to the front with the palm facing in. Hold the right curved hand in the same way near the left, and then draw the right hand in toward the body.

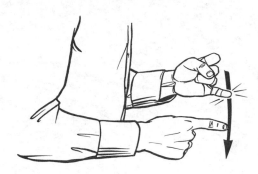

LAST, END
Hold the left hand to the front with the palm facing self and the little finger extended. Strike the left little finger with the right index finger as the right hand moves down.

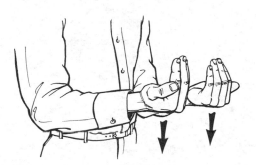

NOW
Hold both bent (or *Y*) hands to the front at waist level with the palms facing up. Drop both hands sharply a short distance.

PAST
Move the right upraised flat hand backward over the right shoulder, with the palm facing the body. The emphasis with which the sign is made can vary, according to the length of time involved.

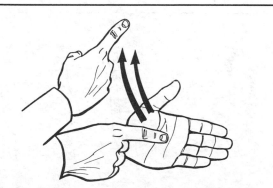

SOMETIMES, ONCE IN A WHILE
Hold the left flat hand at chest level with the palm facing right. Touch the left palm with the tip of the right index finger; then move the right index upward to a vertical position. Repeat after a slight pause.

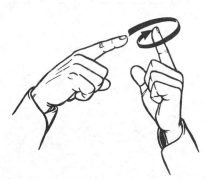

WHEN
Hold the left index finger upright with the palm facing right. Make a clockwise circle around the left index with the right index.

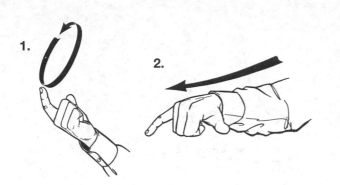

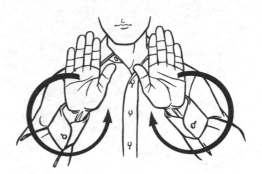

FOREVER
Circle the right index finger with the palm facing up. Then move the right downturned *Y* hand forward.

SUNDAY
Place both flat hands to the front with palms facing forward; then move them at the same time in opposite direction circles. The circles may be made in either direction.

MONDAY
Make a small circle with the right *M* hand.

TUESDAY
Make a small circle with the right *T* hand.

WEDNESDAY
Make a small circle with the right *W* hand.

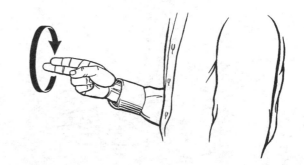

THURSDAY
Make a small circle with the right *H* hand.

FRIDAY
Make a small circle with the right *F* hand.

SATURDAY
Make a small circle with the right *S* hand.

DAY

Point the left index finger to the right, with the palm down. Rest the right elbow on the left index, with the right index pointing up. Move the right index and arm in an arc from right to left across the body.

MONTH

Point the left index finger up, with the palm facing right. Move the right index from the top to the base of the left index.

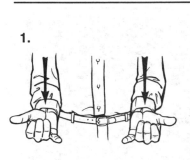

TODAY

Drop both *Y* (or flat) hands in front of the chest. Point the left index finger to the right, with the palm down. Rest the right elbow on the left index and point the right index up. Move the right arm in an arc across the body.

TOMORROW

Touch the right *A* thumb to the right cheek or chin; then make a forward arc with the thumb.

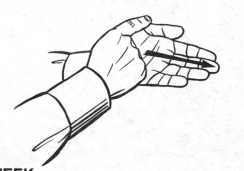

WEEK

Move the right index-finger hand forward across the left flat palm.

YESTERDAY

With the palm facing forward, place the thumb of the right *A* (or *Y*) hand on the right side of the chin. Move the hand in a backward arc toward the ear.

FALL, AUTUMN
Hold the left arm upright with a slight tilt to the right. Move the right index-finger side of the right flat hand down along the left forearm.

SPRING, GROW
Open the fingers of the right *and* hand as they pass up through the left *C* hand.

SUMMER
Draw the right curved index finger across the forehead from left to right.

SUN
Point the right index finger forward and upward just above head level and make a clockwise circle.

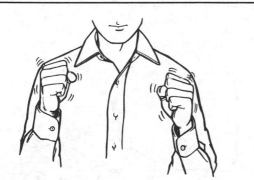

WINTER
Hold up both *S* hands in front of the chest and shake them.

YEAR
Move the right *S* hand in a complete forward circle around the left *S* hand, and end with the right *S* hand on top of the left.

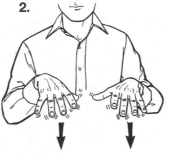

ICE, FREEZE

Hold both open hands to the front with the palms facing down. Curve the fingers and make them rigid while moving the hands down a short distance.

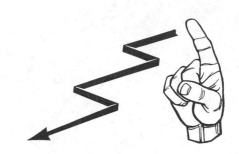

LIGHTNING

Make quick jagged downward movements with the right index finger.

RAIN

Touch the right side of the mouth a couple of times with the right *W* index finger. Then move both open hands down while wiggling the fingers. *Note:* The first part of this sign—*water*—is not always signed.

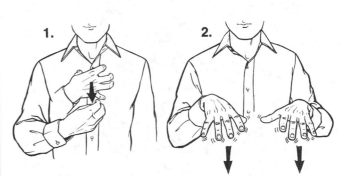

SNOW

Place the fingers and thumb of the right curved hand on the chest; then move the hand forward while forming an *and* hand. Move both palm-down open hands downward while wiggling the fingers.

THUNDER

Point to the right ear with the right index finger; then move both palm-down closed hands alternately forward and backward with forceful action.

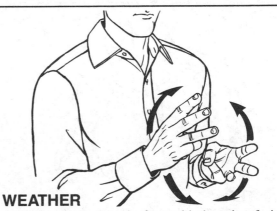

WEATHER

Hold both *W* hands to the front with the palms facing each other; then pivot the hands up and down from the wrists.

AIRPLANE, FLY

Form the right Y hand with the index finger extended and the palm facing down. Make a forward-upward sweeping motion.

CAMERA

Hold both hands with the thumbs and bent index fingers in front of the face. Keep the other fingers closed. Raise and lower the right index finger.

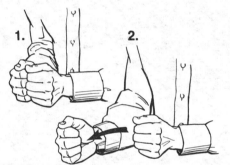

FAR

Move the right A hand well forward from an initial position beside the left A hand.

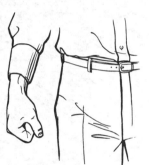

SUITCASE

Use the right hand to imitate the movement of picking up a suitcase.

TRIP, TRAVEL

With the right palm facing down, imitate traveling along a winding road with right curved V fingers.

VISIT

Hold up both V hands, with the palms facing in. Rotate the hands forward alternately.

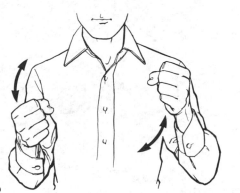

CAR
Use both closed hands to turn an imaginary steering wheel.

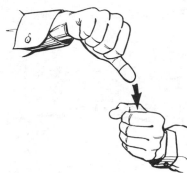
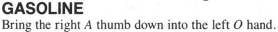

GASOLINE
Bring the right *A* thumb down into the left *O* hand.

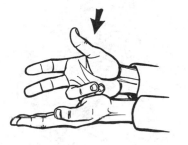

PARK
Bring the right *3* hand down onto the left flat palm. Movements suggesting the parking of a vehicle can also be made with the right *3* hand on the left palm.

RIDE (in a vehicle; verb)
Place the right curved *U* fingers in the left *O* hand and move both hands forward.

STREET, HIGHWAY
Hold both flat hands with the palms facing each other; then move the hands forward together while winding them from side to side.

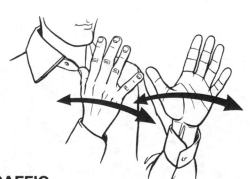

TRAFFIC
With the palms facing each other, move the open hands back and forth a few times.

BOAT
Form a cupped shape with both curved hands, and move the hands forward with a wavy motion.

BRIDGE
Hold the left closed hand to the front with the forearm almost horizontal. Touch the underside of the forearm with the tips of the right *V* fingers, first under the wrist and then under the forearm.

LEAVE
Bring both flat hands up from the right, and close them to *A* hands.

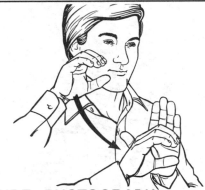

PICTURE, PHOTOGRAPH
Hold the right *C* hand close to the face; then move it forward until the thumb side of the hand is against the left flat palm. The left palm can face either to the right or to the front.

TRAIN
With the palms facing down, rub the fingers of the right *H* hand back and forth over the length of the fingers of the left *H* hand a few times.

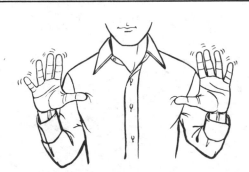

VACATION, HOLIDAY
Place both thumbs at the armpits and wiggle all the fingers.

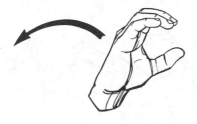

CHRISTMAS
Move the right *C* hand in a sideways arc to the right with the palm facing forward.

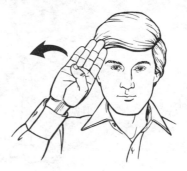

HI
Move the right *B* hand to the right from a position close to the right temple.

HOTEL
Rest the little-finger edge of the right *H* hand on the left index finger while moving the right *H*-hand fingers back and forth.

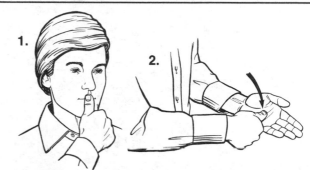

LETTER, MAIL (noun)
Place the right *A* thumb on the mouth and then on the palm of the upturned left hand.

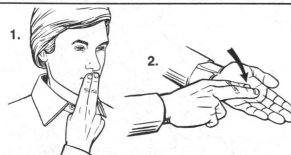

STAMP (postal)
With the palm facing in, touch the lips with the right *U* fingers; then, with the palm facing down, place them on the left palm.

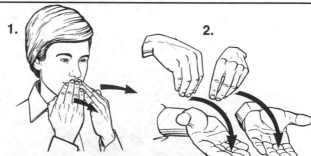

THANKSGIVING
Touch the lips with the fingertips of one or both flat hands; then move the hands forward until the palms are facing up. Hold both curved hands to the front with the palms down; move them forward while forming flat hands that point forward with the palms facing up.

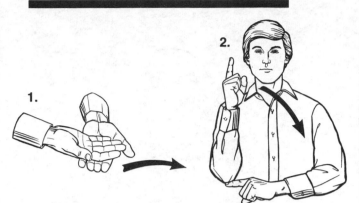

BIRTHDAY, BIRTH, BORN

Place the back of the right flat hand into the left upturned palm. (The right hand may start from a position near the stomach.) Move both hands forward and up together. Add the sign for *day* (page 58). For *birth* and *born*, do not add the sign for *day*.

CELEBRATION

Hold up one or both closed hands with the tips of the thumb and index finger touching. Make small circular movements.

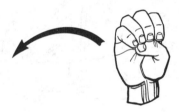

EASTER

Move the right *E* hand in a sideways arc to the right with the palm facing forward.

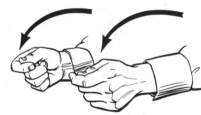

GIFT

With the palms facing each other and the thumb tips touching the inside of each bent index finger, place both closed hands to the front. Move both hands forward in an arc at the same time.

PARADE, MARCH

Swing the fingers of both bent hands back and forth sideways as you move the hands forward, one behind the other.

VALENTINE

Outline a heart shape on the chest with the fingers of both *V* hands.

Travel Puzzle

Read each clue and look at the sign below it. Then fill in the crossword puzzle by spelling out the word corresponding to each sign. (The number 1 in the grid corresponds to the number 1 in the clue, and so on.) Answers are at bottom of page.

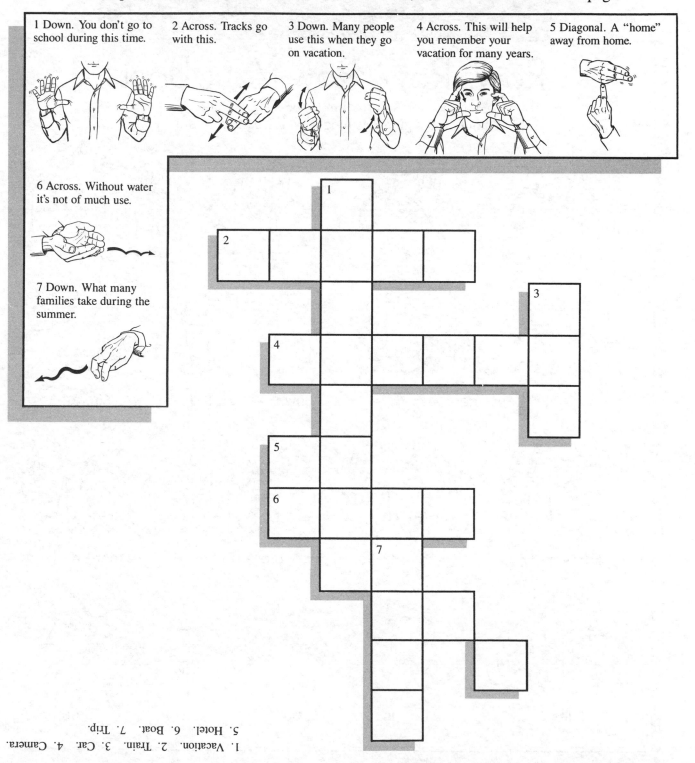

1 Down. You don't go to school during this time.

2 Across. Tracks go with this.

3 Down. Many people use this when they go on vacation.

4 Across. This will help you remember your vacation for many years.

5 Diagonal. A "home" away from home.

6 Across. Without water it's not of much use.

7 Down. What many families take during the summer.

1. Vacation. 2. Train. 3. Car. 4. Camera. 5. Hotel. 6. Boat. 7. Trip.

Row, Row, Row Your Boat

Sign the words in rhythm to the song. Be sure to hold each sign for as long as you sing each word.

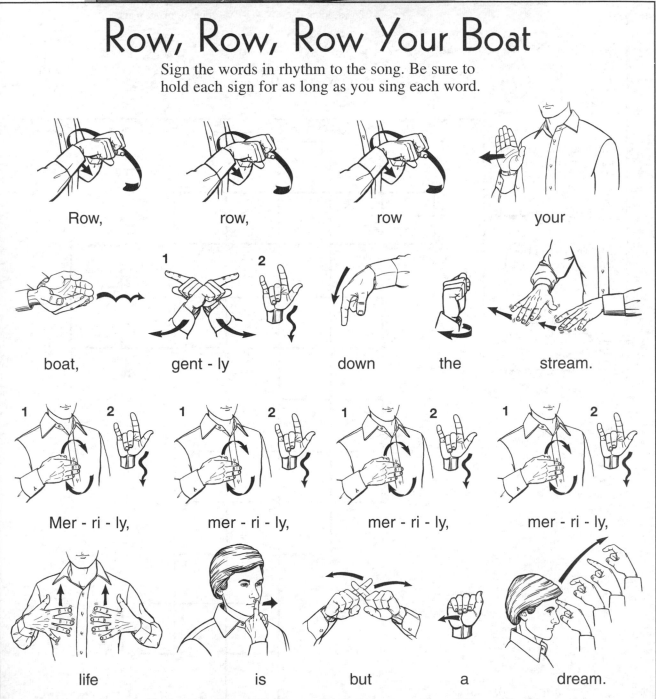

Row,   row,   row   your

boat,   gent - ly   down   the   stream.

Mer - ri - ly,   mer - ri - ly,   mer - ri - ly,   mer - ri - ly,

life   is   but   a   dream.

BLOUSE

Place the thumb side of the right palm-down flat hand on the upper part of the chest. Move the hand down to the waist while turning it so the little-finger edge rests against the body and the palm faces up. Two hands may also be used for this sign.

CLOTHES, DRESS

Brush the fingertips of both flat open hands down the chest a few times.

COAT, JACKET

Move the thumbs of both *A* hands downward from either side of the base of the neck to the center of the lower chest.

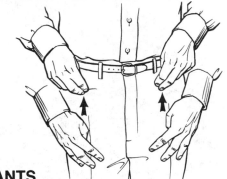

PANTS

Place both curved open hands just below the waist and move them up to the waist while forming *and* hands.

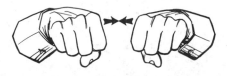

SHOES

Strike the thumb sides of both closed hands together a few times.

SKIRT

Brush the fingers of both flat open hands downward and outward just below the waist.

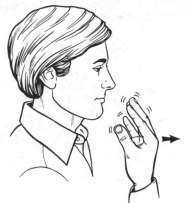

COLOR
Point the fingertips of the right open hand toward the mouth and wiggle them as the hand moves slightly outward.

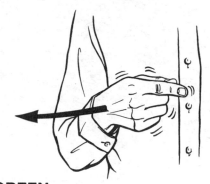

GREEN
Shake the right *G* hand from the wrist while moving it to the right.

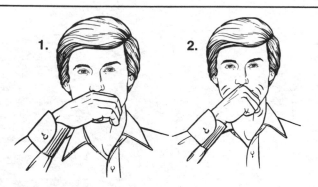

ORANGE (color or fruit)
Open slightly and close the right *S* hand in front of the mouth a few times.

PINK
Stroke downward on the lips with the middle finger of the right *P* hand.

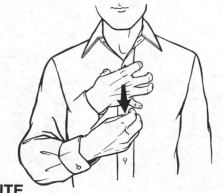

WHITE
Place the fingers and thumb of the right curved hand on the chest; then move the hand forward while forming an *and* hand.

YELLOW
Move the right *Y* hand to the right while shaking it from the wrist.

BLACK
Move the right index finger sideways across the right eyebrow.

BLUE
Move the right *B* hand to the right while shaking it from the wrist.

BROWN
Move the index finger of the right *B* hand down the right cheek.

RED
Stroke downward on the lips with the right index finger (or *R* fingers).

SCISSORS
Open and close the right *H* fingers several times.

TABLE
Place both arms to the front in a position like that of folding them, but put the right forearm over the left. The right flat hand may pat the top of the left forearm a few times.

TELEPHONE, CALL
Position the *Y* hand at the right of the face so that the thumb is near the ear and the little finger near the mouth.

UMBRELLA
Hold the right closed hand over the left closed hand; then raise the right hand a short distance.

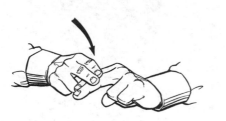

CHAIR, SIT

Place the right *H* fingers on the left *H* fingers, both palms face down. When signing *sit*, move both hands down a little.

HOME

Place the fingertips of the right *and* hand first at the mouth, then at the right cheek. Sometimes the position at the cheek is made with a slightly curved hand.

KEY

Place the right crooked index finger into the left flat palm and twist the index clockwise.

RADIO

Cup both hands over the ears.

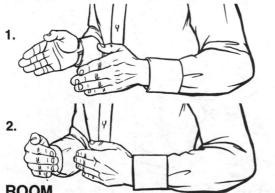

ROOM

Place both flat hands to the front with the palms facing each other; then move the left hand close to the body and the right hand farther away, with both palms facing the body.

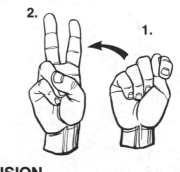

TELEVISION

Fingerspell *T V.*

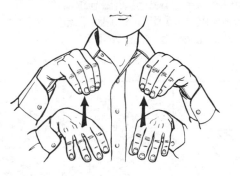

BLANKET

Hold both open hands to the front with the palms facing down and the fingers pointing down. Lift both hands to shoulder level while closing the thumbs on the index fingers.

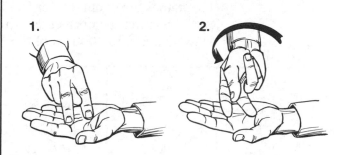

KITCHEN

Place the right *K* hand first palm down, then palm up on the upturned left palm.

MAGAZINE

Move the right thumb and index finger along the little-finger edge of the left flat hand.

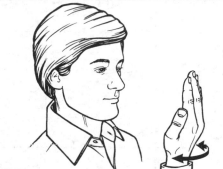

MIRROR

Hold up the slightly curved right hand at eye level, and look at the palm while twisting the hand around slightly from the wrist.

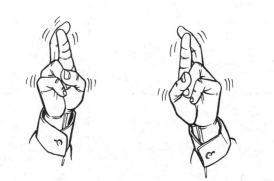

REFRIGERATOR

With the palms facing forward, hold up both *R* hands and shake them.

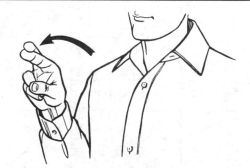

RESTROOM, BATHROOM

Point the right *R* hand forward and move it in a short arc to the right.

Find the Names

How many names can you find in the manual alphabet puzzle below? The names are arranged vertically, horizontally and diagonally. Find out by writing the correct letter in the box near each sign. Some answers are at the bottom of the page.

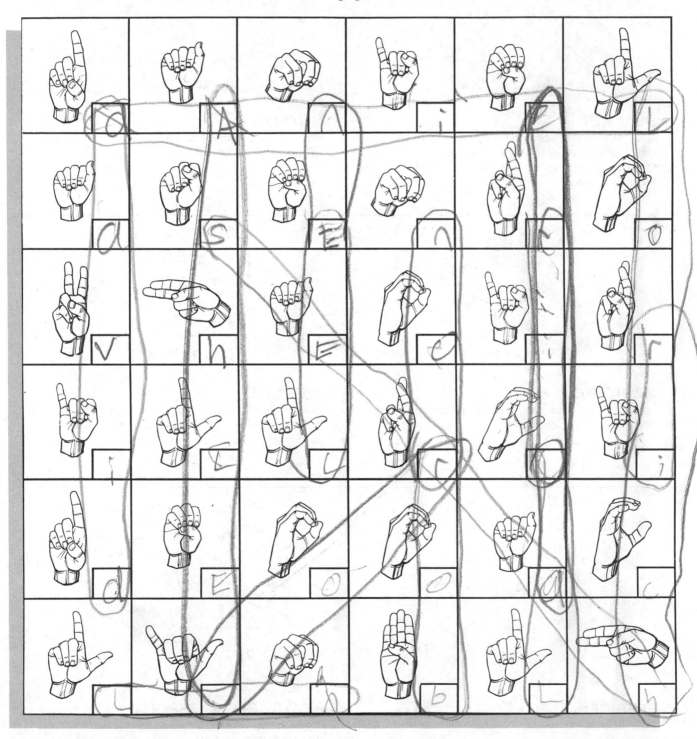

Ashley, Cal, Daniel, David, Erica, Lon, Lori, Lyn, Neal, Niel, Rich, Rob, Ron, Roy, Sarah. (Did you find any more?)

HEALTH & EMERGENCIES 9

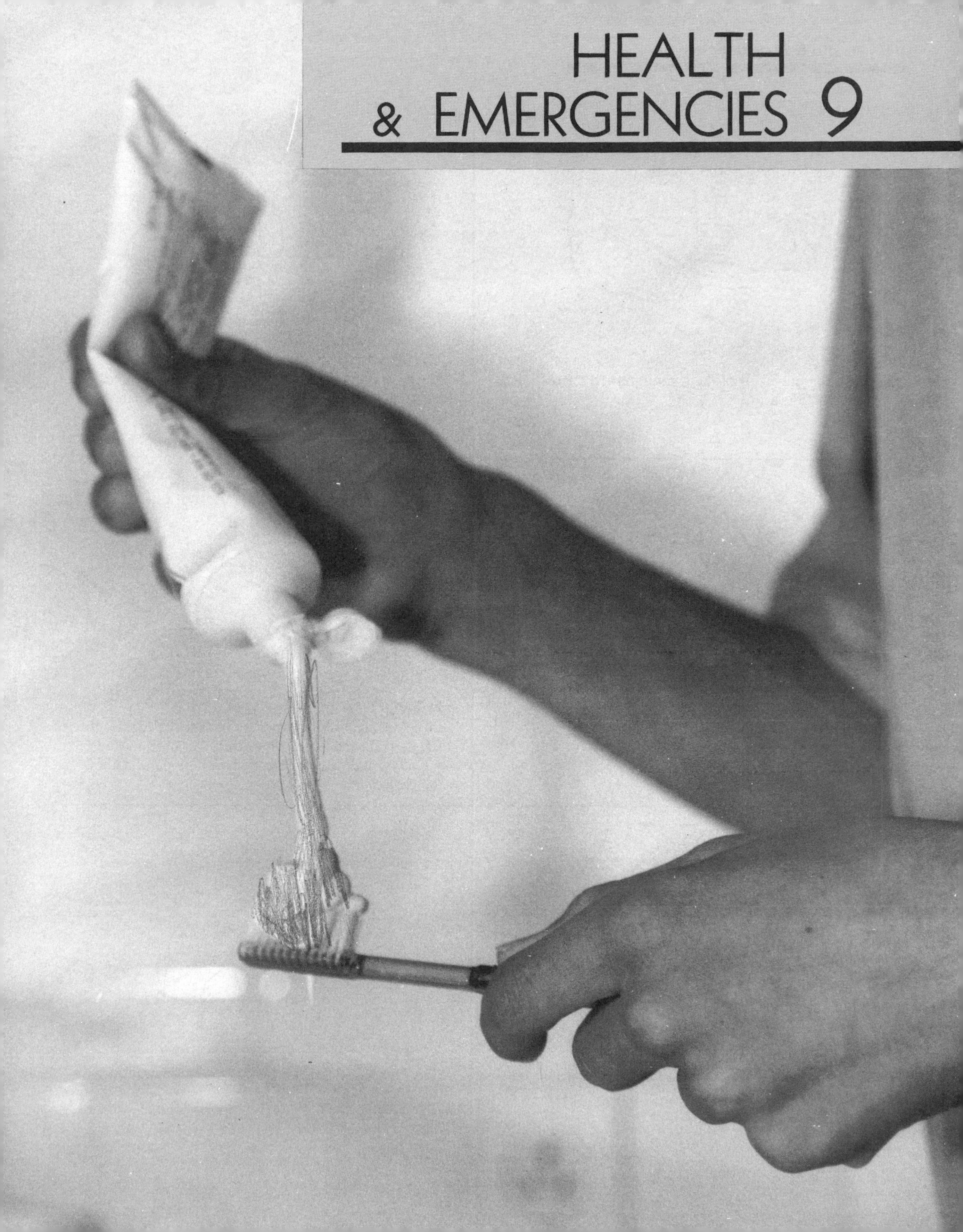

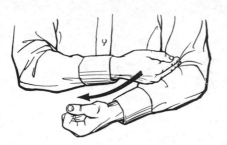

ARM
Move the fingertips of the right upturned curved hand down the left arm.

BODY
Place the palms of both flat hands against the chest and then a little lower. Sometimes only one hand is used.

FEET
Point first to one foot and then to the other.

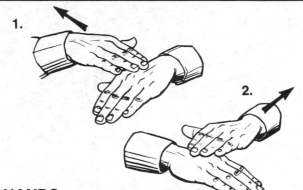

HANDS
Place the right downturned hand over the back of the left downturned hand. Move the right hand toward the body, and repeat the action with the left hand over the right.

HEART (physical)
Place the right middle finger over the heart, with the other fingers extended.

TEETH
Move the tip of the right index finger sideways across the front teeth.

EAR
Touch or point to the right ear with the right index finger.

EYE
Point to the eye with the right index finger.

FACE
Move the right index finger in a counterclockwise direction around the face.

HEAD
Place the fingertips of the right bent hand against the right temple and move the right hand downward in an arc until the fingertips touch the jaw.

MOUTH
Point to the mouth with the right index finger.

NOSE
Touch the tip of the nose with the right index finger.

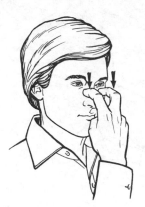

BLIND
Place the tips of the right curved *V* fingers in front of the eyes and lower them slightly. Sometimes the eyes are closed.

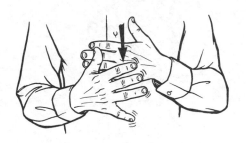

BLOOD, BLEED
Wiggle the fingers of the right open hand as they move down the back of the left open hand.

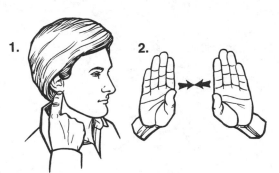

DEAF
Touch or point to the right ear with the right index finger. Place both flat hands to the front and slightly apart with palms forward. Move them together until the index fingers and thumbs touch.

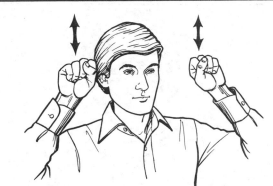

EXERCISE
Hold both *S* hands up to the front with the palms facing forward. Move both hands up and down (or forward and backward) at the same time.

HEARING
Place the right index finger in front of the mouth and make a few small forward circular movements.

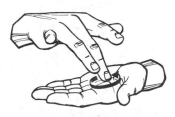

MEDICINE
Make small circles on the left palm with the right middle finger.

BATH
Rub both *A* hands up and down on the chest several times.

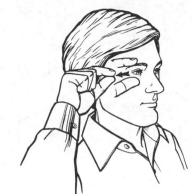

GLASSES
Place the fingers and thumb of the right *G* hand above and below the right eye, at the side of the head. Move the fingers back to the ear while closing them.

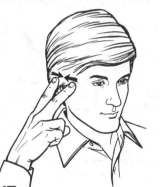

HAIRCUT
Open and close the right *H* fingers near the hair several times.

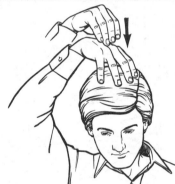

SHOWER
Place the closed *S* (or *and*) hand above the head; drop the hand down toward the head while opening the hand.

SLEEP, NAP
Place the palm side of the right open hand in front of the face and move it down to chin level while forming an *and* hand.

TOOTHBRUSH
Move the right horizontal index finger up and down in front of the teeth.

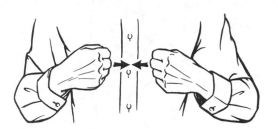

ACCIDENT
Strike the knuckles of both clenched hands together.

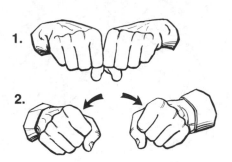

BREAK
Hold the thumb and index-finger sides of both *S* hands together; then twist them sharply outward and apart.

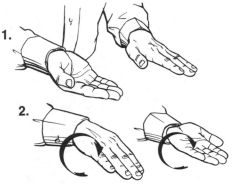

DEATH, DEAD, DIE
Hold both flat hands to the front with the right palm facing up and the left palm facing down. Move both hands in an arc to the left while changing the hand positions so that the palms reverse direction.

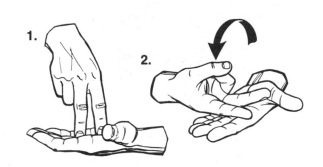

FALL
Stand the right *V* fingers in the left flat palm. Flip them over so that the backs of the *V* fingers rest on the left palm.

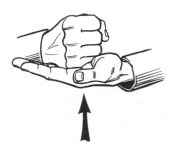

HELP
Place the right closed hand on the left flat palm and lift both hands together.

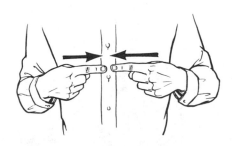

HURT, PAIN
Push the index fingers toward each other several times. This may be done near the area of the body that is feeling pain.

DANGER
Hold the left closed hand to the front with the palm facing the body and the arm pointing right. Move the back of the right *A* thumb up across the back of the left hand a few times.

HOSPITAL
With the fingers of the right *H* hand draw a cross on the upper left arm.

OPERATION
Move the thumbnail of the right *A* hand down (or across) the chest or stomach.

POISON
Make small circles on the left palm with the middle finger of the right *P* hand.

SHOT (injection)
Place the right curved thumb, index and middle finger at the upper left arm and move the thumb toward the fingers.

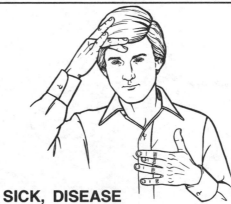

SICK, DISEASE
Place the right middle finger on the forehead and the left middle finger on the stomach.

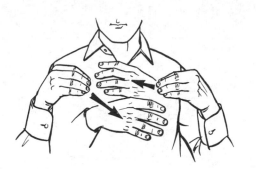

AFRAID, SCARED
Move both *and* hands from the sides in opposite directions across the chest at the same time. During the movement, change the hand positions to open hands.

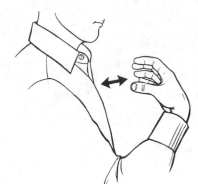

COUGH
Strike the chest sharply a few times with the fingertips of the right curved open hand.

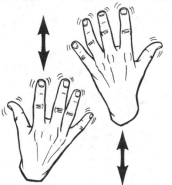

FIRE, BURN
With the palms facing in, move both slightly curved open hands up and down alternately in front of the body while wiggling the fingers.

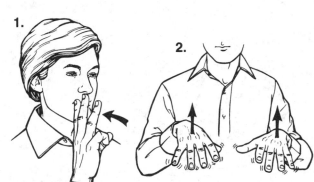

FLOOD
Touch the mouth with the index finger of the right *W* hand a few times (the sign for *water*). Point both palm-down open hands forward and raise them while wiggling the fingers.

HURRY
Move one or both *H* hands quickly forward in short arcs. If two hands are used, they can be quickly moved up and down alternately.

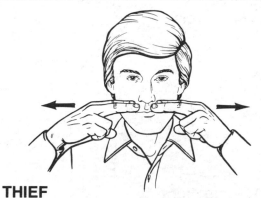

THIEF
Place the index-finger side of both *H* hands under the nose; then draw both hands outward.

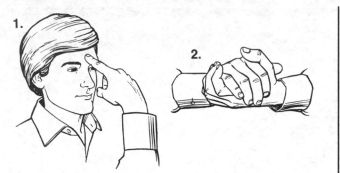

BELIEVE
Touch the forehead with the right index finger; then bring the right hand down until it clasps the left hand in front of the chest.

CHURCH
Place the thumb of the right *C* hand on the back of the left closed hand.

FORGIVE
Stroke the lower part of the left flat hand with the right fingertips several times.

GOSPEL
Slide the little-finger edge of the right *G* hand across the left flat hand from fingertips to heel a few times.

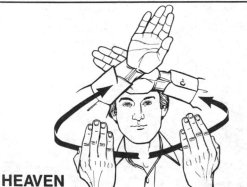

HEAVEN
Hold both flat hands out in front with the fingers pointing up and the palms facing the body. Make a circle with both hands toward the body; then pass the right hand under the left palm and up as the hands are crossed at forehead level.

PEACE
Place the right flat hand on the left flat hand at chest level; then place the left on the right. Next move both flat hands down and to the sides, with the palms down. Pass from one position to another smoothly.

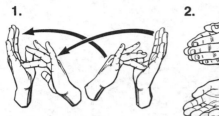 

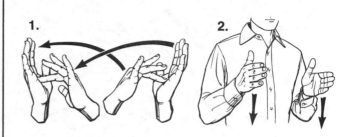

BIBLE

Hold both open hands to the front with the palms facing each other. Touch the left palm with the right middle finger; then touch the right palm with the left middle finger. Place hands palm to palm, with fingers pointing forward. Open both hands to palm-up position while keeping edges of little fingers together.

CHRISTIAN

Hold both open slightly curved hands to the front, palms facing each other. Touch the left palm with the right middle finger; then touch the right palm with the left middle finger. Add the *person* ending: hold both flat open hands to the front, palms facing each other; then move the hands down at the same time.

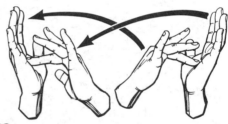

GOD

Point the right *G* finger in a forward-upward direction at head level. Move right hand in a backward-downward arc toward self, ending with a *B* hand in front of upper chest with palm still facing left.

JESUS

Hold both open slightly curved hands to the front with the palms facing each other. Touch the left palm with the right middle finger; then touch the right palm with the left middle finger.

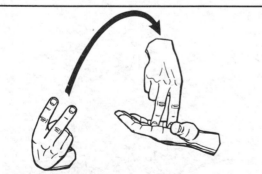

RESURRECTION

Hold the left flat hand to the front with the palm facing up. Bring the right *V* hand up from a palm-up position until the *V* fingers stand on the left palm.

WORSHIP

Close the left hand over the right closed hand and move both hands slowly toward the body. Bow head slightly.

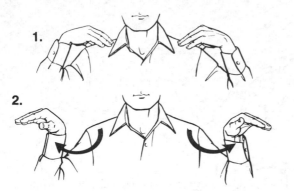

ANGEL
Touch the shoulders with the fingertips of both hands (sometimes only one hand is used). Point the fingers of both downturned hands outward to the sides; then flap the hands up and down a few times.

BAPTIZE
Hold both *A* hands to the front with the palms facing each other. Move both hands to the right and down slightly, and at the same time turn the hands so that the thumbs point to the right.

HOLY
Make a right *H* hand; then move the right flat palm across the left flat palm from heel to fingertips.

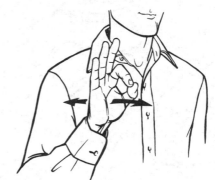

MINISTER
Place the right *F* hand in front of the right shoulder, with the palm facing forward. Move the hand forward and backward a few times.

PRAY, PRAYER
Place both flat hands to the front with the palms touching; then move them toward the body, and at the same time move the head slightly forward.

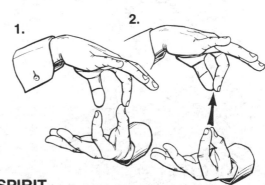

SPIRIT
Bring the right open hand down toward the left open hand with the palms facing each other. Form *F* hands as the right hand is drawn up.

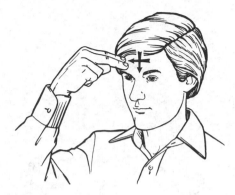

CATHOLIC
Outline a cross in front of the forehead with the right *U* fingers. Move hand first down, then from left to right.

JEWISH
Place the right open fingers and thumb on the chin with the palm facing the body. Draw the hand down below the chin and form an *and* hand.

PASSOVER
Tap the left elbow with the right *P* fingers a few times.

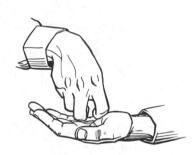

PROTESTANT, KNEEL
Imitate kneeling legs with the fingers of the right *V* hand on the left flat palm.

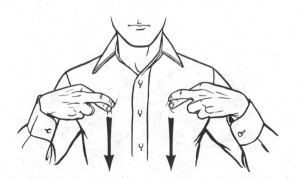

RABBI
With the palms facing the body, place the fingertips of the *R* hands on the chest. Move both hands at the same time down toward the stomach.

TEMPLE (building)
Place the heel of the right *T* hand on the back of the left closed hand.

DEVIL

Touch the temple with the thumb of the right palm-forward *3* hand. Bend and unbend the index and middle fingers a few times.

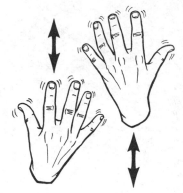

HELL

With the palms facing in, move both slightly curved open hands up and down alternately in front of the body while wiggling the fingers.

MEDITATE

Make forward circles near the right temple with the right *M* hand.

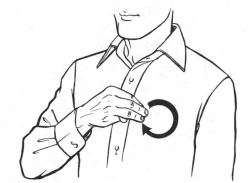

MISSIONARY

Make a counterclockwise circle over the heart with the right *M* hand.

RELIGION

Place the right *R* fingers on the heart and move the hand in a forward-upward arc; end with the palm facing forward.

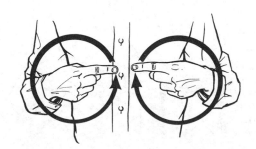

SIN, EVIL

Point both index fingers toward each other, with the palms facing the body. Move both index fingers at the same time in up-out-down-in circles.

EASY, SIMPLE
Hold the left curved hand to the front with the palm up. Brush the little-finger edge of the right curved hand upward over the fingertips of the left hand several times.

HARD, DIFFICULT
Strike the knuckles of both bent *V* hands while moving them up and down.

GOOD
Place the fingers of the right flat hand at the lips; then move the right hand down into the palm of the left, with both palms facing up.

BAD
Place the fingertips of the right flat hand at the lips; then move the right hand down and turn it so that the palm faces down.

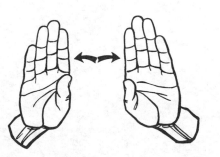

OPEN
Place the thumbs and index fingers of both flat hands together, with the palms facing forward. (Some prefer the palms facing down.) Move both hands sideways in opposite directions.

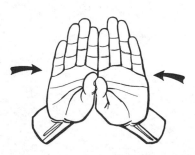

CLOSE, SHUT
With palms facing forward, bring both flat hands together from the sides.

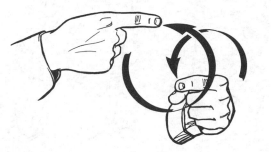

COME
Point both index fingers toward each other, and circle them around each other while moving them toward the body.

GO
Point both index fingers toward each other, and circle them around each other while moving them away from the body.

BEAUTIFUL
Place the fingertips of the right *and* hand at the chin and open the hand as it describes a counterclockwise circle around the face.

UGLY
Cross the index fingers just below the nose, with the remaining fingers closed; then pull the hands apart to the sides while bending the index fingers.

CLEAN
Move the palm of the right flat hand across the palm of the left flat hand from wrist to fingertips.

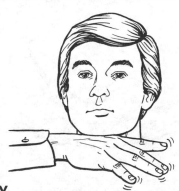

DIRTY
Place the back of the right hand under the chin and wiggle the fingers.

DRY

Move the right curved index finger from left to right across the lips.

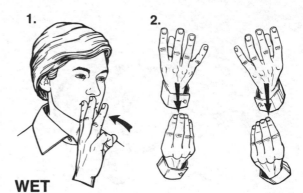

WET

Tap the right side of the mouth with the index finger of the right *W* hand a few times. Hold both curved open hands to the front with the palms facing up; then move the hands slowly down while forming *and* hands.

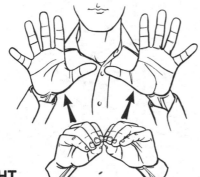

LIGHT

Hold both *and* hands at chest level with the palms down. Open the hands while moving them up and to the sides, with the palms facing forward.

DARK

Cross the palms of both flat hands down in front of the face.

NEW

Pass the back of the right slightly curved hand across the left flat palm from fingers to heel. Continue the movement of the right hand in a slightly upward direction.

OLD

Close the right hand just below the chin and move the hand downward.

SAME
Bring the index fingers together, with the palms facing down.

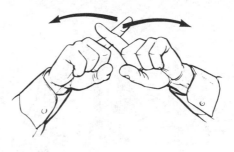

DIFFERENT
Cross both index fingers, with the palms facing out; then draw the fingers apart beyond the width of the body.

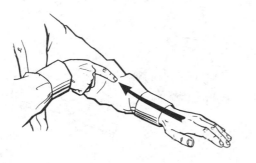

LONG
Extend the left flat hand to the front with the palm facing down. Run the right index finger up the left arm, beginning at the fingertips.

SHORT, SOON
Cross the fingers of both *H* hands and rub the right *H* hand back and forth over the left index finger from fingertip to knuckle.

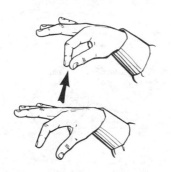

FIND, DISCOVER
Hold the right open hand in front with the palm facing down; then bring the index and thumb together while raising the hand.

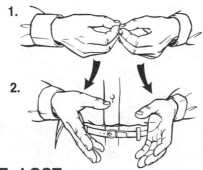

LOSE, LOST
Hold the fingertips of both palm-up *and* hands together; then separate the hands by dropping them down and opening them.

EXCITING
Stroke the chest a few times, using both middle fingers alternately with a forward circular motion. Extend the other fingers.

BORING
Touch the side of the nose with the right index finger and twist the finger forward slightly.

BIG, LARGE
Hold both *L* hands to the front with the palms facing each other. Move the hands outward to the sides, beyond the width of the body.

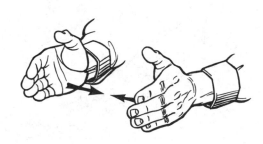

SMALL, LITTLE
Hold both flat hands to the front with the palms facing each other. Move the hands closer to each other in short stages.

YES
Nod the right *S* hand up and down with the palm facing forward.

NO
Bring the right thumb, index and middle finger together.

START, BEGIN
Hold the left flat hand forward with the palm facing right. Place the tip of the right index finger between the left index and middle finger; then twist the right index in a clockwise direction once or twice.

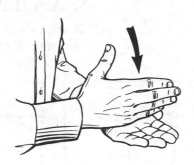

STOP
Bring the little-finger side of the right flat hand down sharply at right angles on the left palm.

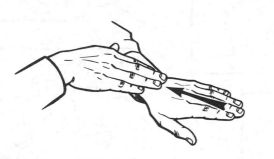

SLOW
Draw the right hand slowly upward over the back of the left hand. Begin near the fingertips and move up to the wrist.

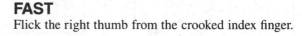

FAST
Flick the right thumb from the crooked index finger.

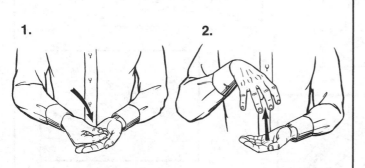

RICH, WEALTHY
Put the back of the right *and* hand in the upturned palm of the left hand; then lift the right above the left while forming a curved open hand with the palm facing down.

POOR
Place the right curved hand under the left elbow and pull the fingers and thumb down into the *and* position a few times.

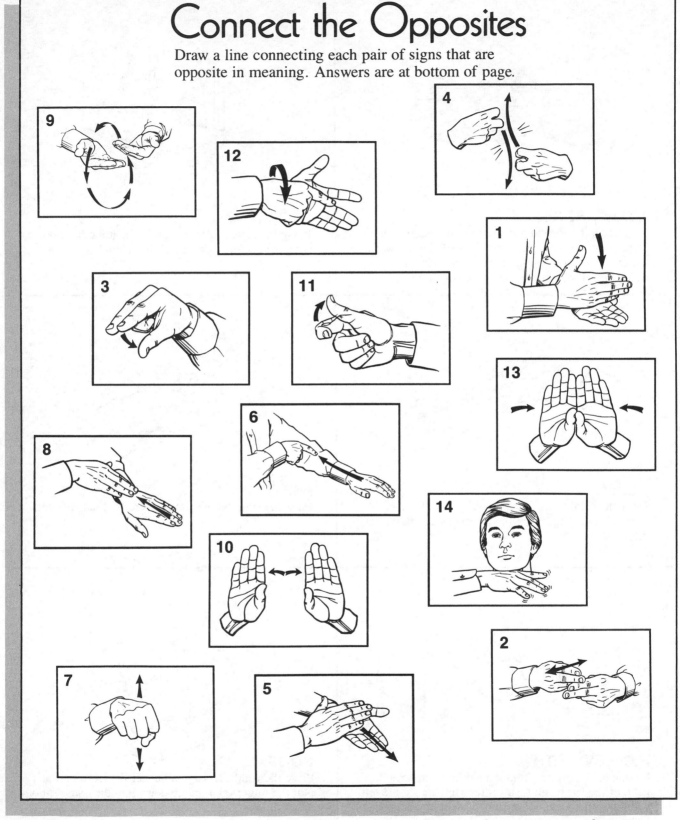

Connect the Opposites

Draw a line connecting each pair of signs that are opposite in meaning. Answers are at bottom of page.

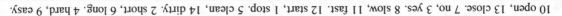

10 open, 13 close, 7 no, 3 yes, 8 start, 12 fast, 11 slow, 1 stop, 5 clean, 14 dirty, 2 short, 6 long, 4 hard, 9 easy.

ANSWER
Hold the right index finger to the lips and place the left index finger a short distance in front of the right. Move both hands forward and down from the wrists so that the index fingers point forward.

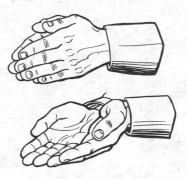

BOOK
Place the hands palm to palm, with the fingers pointing forward. Open both hands to the palm-up position while keeping the edges of the little fingers together.

LEARN
Place the fingers of the right open hand on the left upturned palm. Close the right fingers as the hand is moved to the forehead. Then touch the fingertips to the forehead.

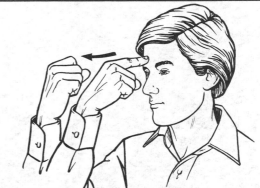

MEMORIZE
Touch the right index finger to the center of the forehead; then move the right hand forward from the forehead to an S position, with the palm facing in.

READ
Point the right V fingers at the left flat palm and move them downward.

WRITE
Touch the right index finger and thumb, with the other fingers closed; then move the right hand across the left flat palm with a slight wavy motion.

LESSON
Place the little-finger edge of the right flat hand across the fingers of the left flat hand. Move the right hand in a small arc so that it rests at the base of the left hand.

PAPER
Strike the heel of the left upturned palm with two quick motions of the heel of the right downturned palm. The right hand moves from right to left.

SCHOOL
Clap the hands two or three times.

STUDY
Point the right open fingers toward the left flat hand. Move the right hand back and forth a short distance from the left while wiggling the right fingers.

TEACH
Position both open *and* hands at the front and sides of the head; then move the hands forward while forming closed *and* hands.

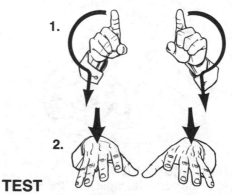

TEST
Hold up both index fingers and with each draw the shape of a question mark, in opposite directions; then open both hands and move them forward.

AMERICAN SIGN LANGUAGE, ASL, AMESLAN

Rotate both *A* hands alternately toward the body, with the palms facing forward. Then point both *L* hands toward each other and move them to the sides with a twisting motion from the wrists.

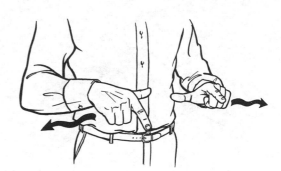

LANGUAGE

Point both *L* hands toward each other (sometimes the index fingers point up), and move them to the sides with a twisting motion from the wrists.

LIBRARY

Make a small clockwise circle with the right *L* hand.

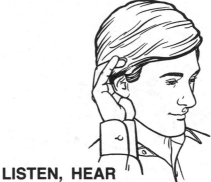

LISTEN, HEAR

Place the right cupped hand behind the right ear and turn the head a little to the left.

SIGN (the language of)

Hold both index fingers to the front with the fingers pointing toward each other and the palms facing out. Rotate both index fingers alternately toward the body.

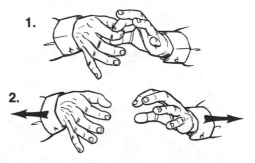

STORY

Link the thumbs and index fingers of both *F* hands and pull them apart several times.

DICTIONARY
Hold up the right *D* hand and shake it.

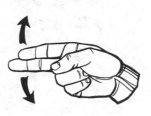

HISTORY
Shake the right *H* hand up and down a short distance.

NURSE
Place the right extended *N* fingertips on the left upturned wrist.

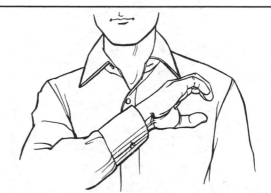

POLICE, COP, SHERIFF
Place the thumb side of the right *C* hand at the left shoulder.

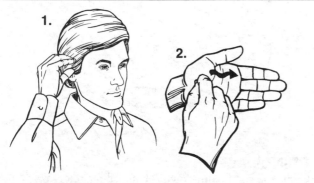

SECRETARY
Remove an imaginary pencil from above the right ear, and mimic handwriting action on the left flat hand.

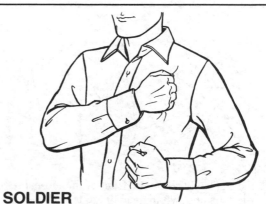

SOLDIER
Place the palm side of the right *A* hand just below the left shoulder and the palm side of the left *A* hand several inches below the right hand.

DENTIST
Touch the teeth with the thumb of the right *D* hand.

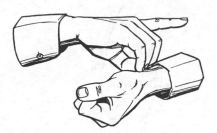

DOCTOR
Place the right *D* hand or *M* fingers on the upturned left wrist.

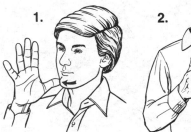

FARMER
With the thumb on the chin, drag the right open hand, palm facing left, from left to right across the chin. Add the *person* ending by holding both flat open hands to the front with the palms facing each other; then move the hands down at the same time.

JOB, WORK
With the palms facing down, tap the wrist of the right *S* hand on the wrist of the left *S* hand a few times.

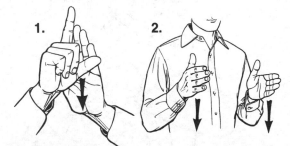

LAWYER, LAW
Place the right *L* hand on the front of the left palm. Move the *L* hand down in a small arc to the base of the left hand. For *lawyer*, add the *person* ending by holding both flat open hands to the front, palms facing each other; then move the hands down at the same time. Do not use the *person* ending for *law*.

PRINCIPAL
Circle the right palm-down *P* hand counterclockwise over the back of the left flat hand.

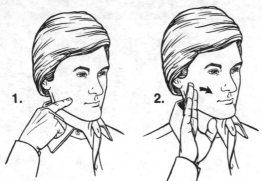

BEE
Touch the right cheek with the right index finger. Quickly brush the index-finger side of the right flat hand downward across the cheek.

FLOWER
Place the fingertips of the right *and* hand under each nostril separately.

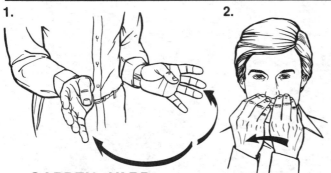

GARDEN, YARD
Hold the horizontal open hands close together with the palms facing in. Make a half-circle with each hand toward the body until bases of palms meet. Place the fingertips of the right *and* hand under each nostril separately.

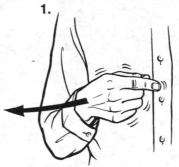
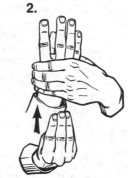

GRASS
Shake the right *G* hand from the wrist while moving it to the right; then open the fingers of the right *and* hand as they pass up through the left *C* hand.

TREE
Place the right elbow in the left palm, with the right fingers pointing up. Turn the right wrist and wiggle the fingers.

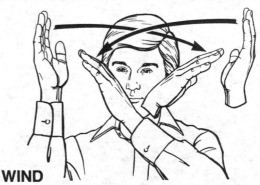

WIND
Hold both open hands up at head level with the palms facing each other. Sweep the hands back and forth from left to right a few times.

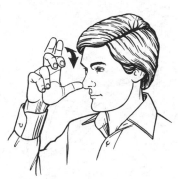

BUG, INSECT
Touch the nose with the thumb tip of the right *3* hand. Bend and unbend the index and middle finger a few times.

BUTTERFLY
Hook the thumbs of both open hands in the crossed position in front of the chest with the palms facing the body. Wiggle the fingers and flap the hands.

FLY (insect)
Move the right flat hand quickly onto the left forearm. End with the right hand closed.

FROG
Hold the right closed hand under the chin with the palm facing in. Flick out the right index and middle finger.

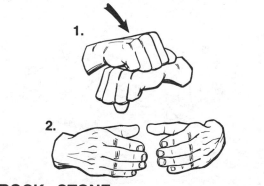

ROCK, STONE
Strike the right closed hand on the back of the left closed hand; then hold both *C* hands slightly apart with the palms facing each other.

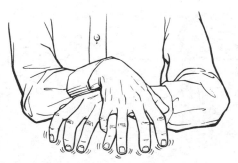

SPIDER
With the palms facing down, hook the little fingers of both curved open hands. Move the hands forward while wiggling the fingers.

EARTH
Grasp the back of the left closed hand between the right index and thumb, and turn the right hand from left to right (toward the left fingers and elbow).

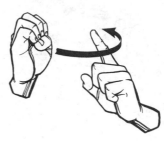

ENVIRONMENT
Circle the right *E* hand counterclockwise around the front of the left vertical index finger.

LAND
Hold both curved hands to the front with the palms facing up, and rub the fingertips with the thumbs. Make circles in opposite directions with downturned flat hands.

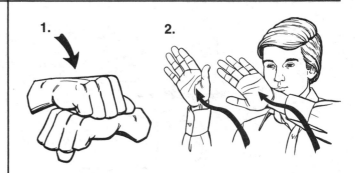

MOUNTAIN, HILL
Strike the right closed hand on the back of the left closed hand (the sign for *rock*); then move both open hands upward to the front with a wavy motion. For *hill* do not sign *rock*.

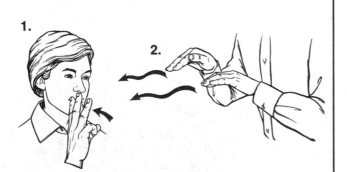

OCEAN, SEA
Touch the mouth with the index finger of the right *W* hand a few times (the sign for *water*). Move both downturned curved hands forward with a wavy motion.

PLANT
Move the right downturned curved hand from left to right while moving the right thumb across the inside of the fingers from little finger to index.

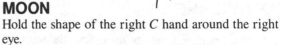

CLOUD

Hold both open curved hands to the front at head level with the palms facing each other. Move both hands from one side to the other while making circular and up-and-down movements from the wrists.

MOON

Hold the shape of the right *C* hand around the right eye.

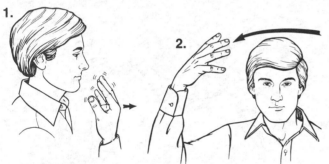

RAINBOW

Point the fingertips of the right open hand toward the mouth and wiggle them as the hand moves slightly outward (the sign for *color*). Move the right open hand over the head in an arc from left to right.

RIVER

Touch the mouth with the index finger of the right *W* hand a few times (the sign for *water*). Place both open hands with the palms facing down and wiggle the fingers as both hands move either to the right or to the left.

SKY

Hold the right flat hand slightly above head level with the palm facing in. Move the hand in an arc from left to right.

WORLD

Make a forward circle with the right *W* hand around the left *W* hand. End with the little-finger edge of the right *W* hand resting on the thumb side of the left *W* hand.

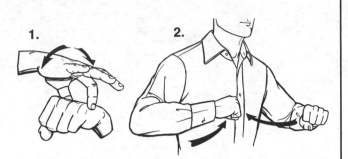

EARTHQUAKE

Grasp the back of the left closed hand between the right index finger and thumb; then move the right hand back and forth. Move both fists forward and backward in front of the body with forceful movements as if pounding the chest.

INVENT, CREATE

With the palm facing left, touch the forehead with the right index finger of the *4* hand. Beginning with the fingertip, push the length of the index finger upward on the forehead with a slight forward curve.

ROCKET, MISSILE

Place the right *R* hand on the back of the left downturned closed hand, and move the right hand forward and up.

SCIENCE

Place both *A* hands in front of the shoulders and move the hands alternately in and down a few times.

STAR

Point both index fingers upward at eye level. Move them alternately upward, striking the side of one index finger against the other.

UNIVERSE

Make a forward circle with the right *U* hand around the left *U* hand. End with the little-finger edge of the right *U* hand resting on the thumb side of the left *U* hand.

COMPUTER

Move the right *C* hand in a double arc from right to left in front of the forehead with palm facing left. *Note:* See alternative sign for *computer* on page 132.

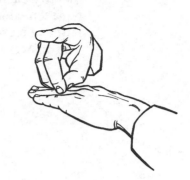

DIAMOND

Place the thumb and middle finger of the right *D* hand on the fourth finger of the left hand which faces down.

ORBIT

Move the right index finger in a forward circle once around the left *S* hand. End with the right index finger on top of the left *S* hand.

GOLD

Touch the right ear with the right index finger. Shake the right *Y* hand as it moves down and forward.

WOOD

Move the edge of the right flat hand back and forth over the the back of the left flat hand a couple times.

SILVER

Touch the right ear with the right index finger. Move the right hand forward to an *S* hand and shake it.

Find the Message

Identify each sign of the manual alphabet
represented below the grid. Then write the letter
in the corresponding numbered box of the grid.
The answer is at the bottom of the page.

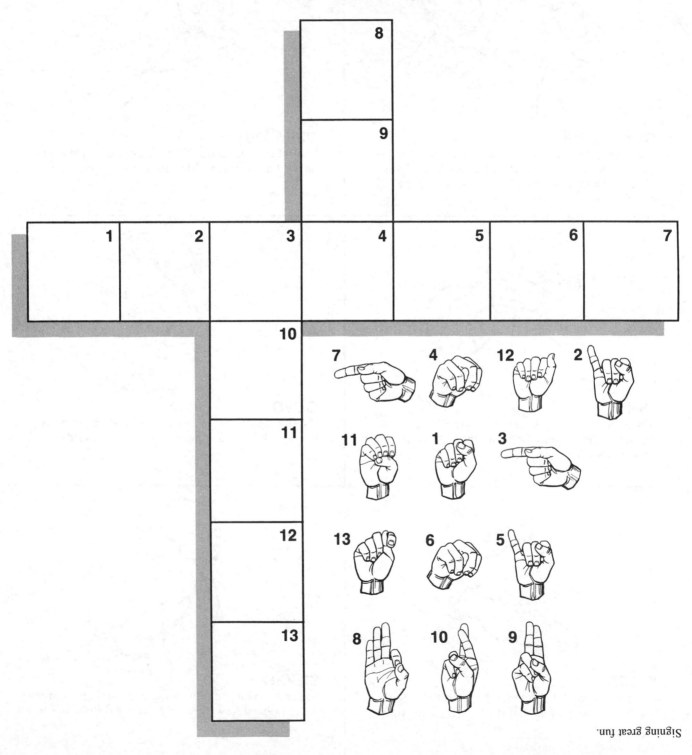

Signing great fun.

THOUGHTS & FEELINGS 14

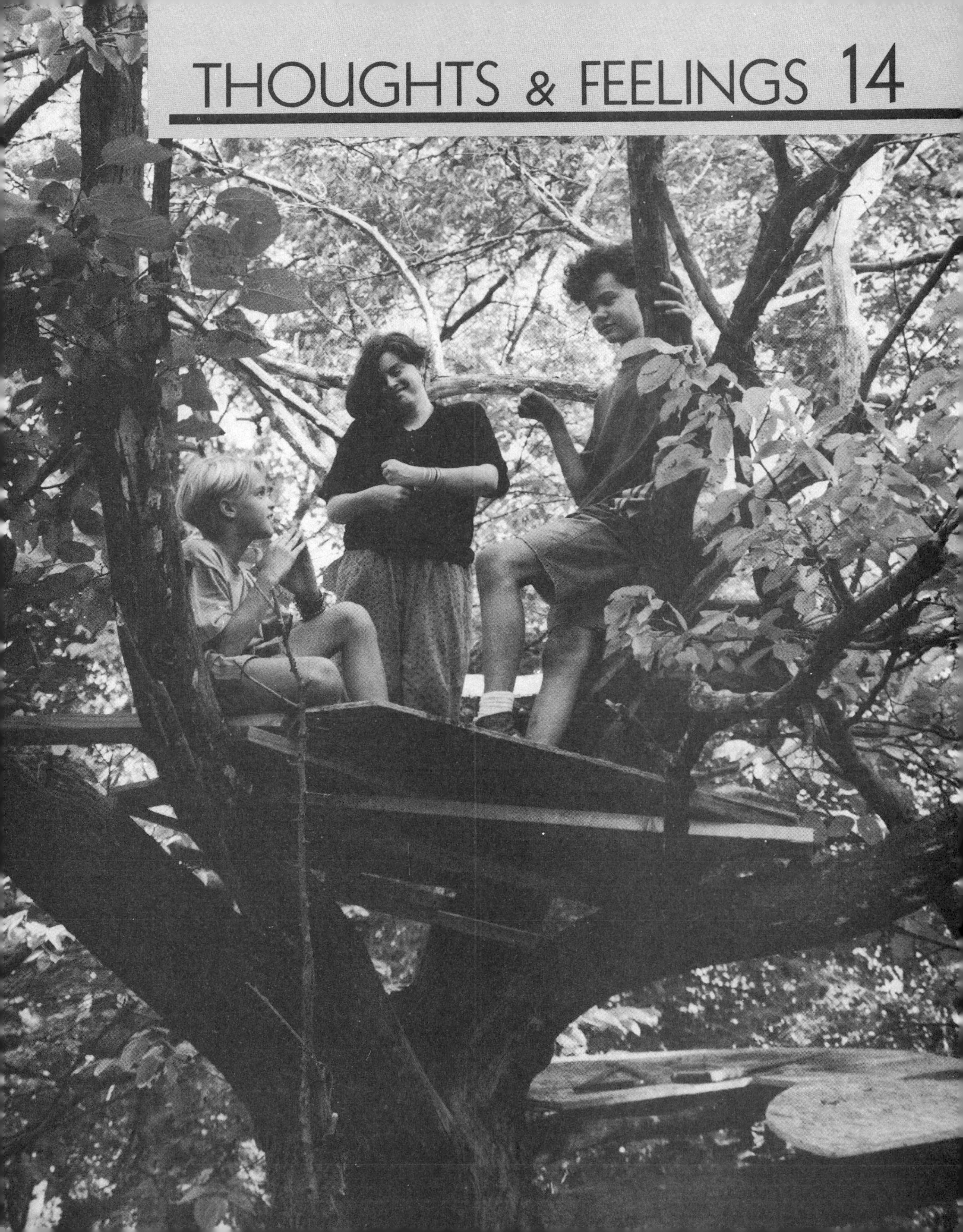

DREAM, DAYDREAM
Touch the forehead with the right index finger and move the hand upward and forward while bending and unbending the index finger.

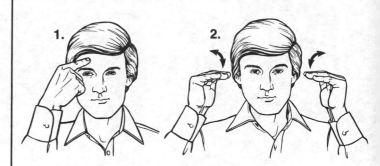

HOPE
Touch the forehead with the right index finger; then bring both flat hands before the chest or head, with the palms facing each other. Bend and unbend the hands at the same time, twice.

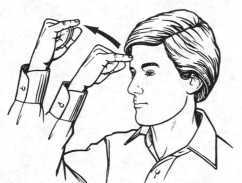

IDEA
Place the little finger of the right *I* hand on the forehead, with the palm facing in. Move the hand forward and upward.

KNOW
Tap the fingers of the right slightly curved hand on the forehead a few times.

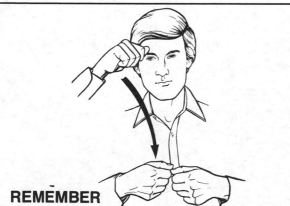

REMEMBER
Touch the thumb of the right *A* hand to the forehead; then place it on top of the thumb of the left *A* hand.

THINK
Make a counterclockwise circle just in front of the forehead with the right index finger.

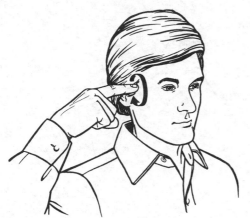

CRAZY

Point the right index finger to the temple and make a few small circles.

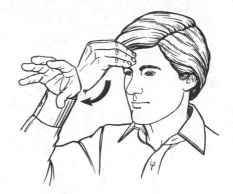

DON'T CARE

Touch the fingers of the closed *and* hand to the forehead; then flick the hand forward while opening the fingers.

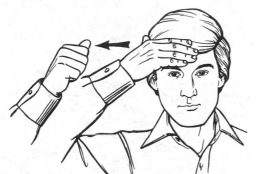

FORGET

Wipe the palm side of the right open hand from left to right across the forehead. End with the right hand in the *A* position close to the right temple.

GUESS

Move the right *C* hand from right to left across the face and close in a downturned *S* position.

SECRET

Place the thumb of the right *A* hand over the lips a few times.

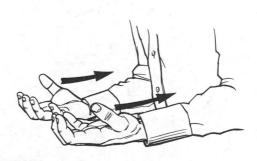

WANT

With palms up, move both open curved hands toward the body a few times.

ANGRY

Place the fingertips of both curved hands against the stomach and draw the hands forcefully up to the chest with slight inward curves.

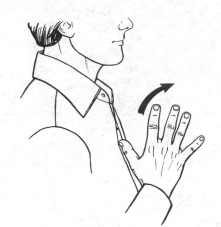

FINE

Place the thumb edge of the right flat open hand at the chest and then move the hand slightly up and forward.

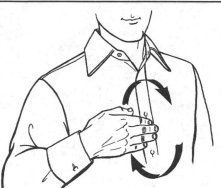

HAPPY

Move the right flat hand in forward circles as the palm touches the chest.

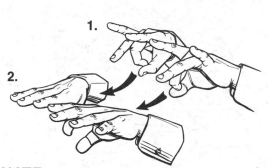

HATE

Hold both open hands in front of the chest with the palms facing down, and flick both middle fingers outward.

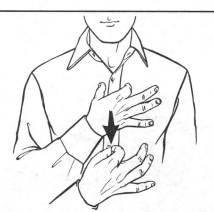

LIKE

Place the right thumb and index finger against the chest, with the other fingers extended. Bring the thumb and index finger together as the hand is moved a short distance forward.

SAD

With the palms facing in, bend the head forward slightly while dropping the open hands down the length of the face.

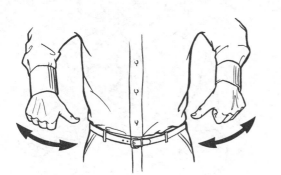

BRAG, SHOW OFF
Move one or both *A*-hand thumbs in and out at the sides just above the waist.

CRY, TEARS
Move one or both index fingers down the cheeks from underneath the eyes a few times.

EMBARRASS
Raise and lower both open hands alternately in front of the face, with the palms facing in.

LAUGH
Starting near the corners of the mouth, move both index fingers upward over the cheeks a few times.

LONELY
Hold the right index finger in front of the lips, with the palm facing left. Move the index finger down across the lips a few times.

SELFISH
Point both *V* hands forward, with the palms facing down; then pull the hands in toward the body while bending the *V* fingers.

FEELING
Move the right middle finger upward on the chest, with the other fingers extended.

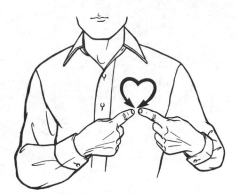

HEART (emotional)
Outline the shape of a heart on the chest with both index or middle fingers.

JEALOUS
Put the tip of the right little finger at the corner of the mouth and give it a twist.

KISS
Place the fingers of the right hand on the lips and then on the cheek.

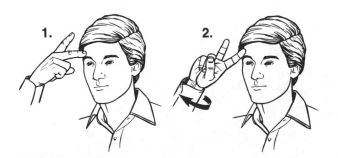

MISUNDERSTAND
Put the right *V* hand to the forehead, touching first with the middle finger, then twisting the hand and touching with the index finger.

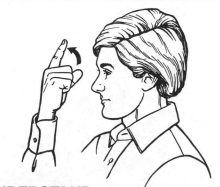

UNDERSTAND
With the palm facing in, flick the right index finger up vertically in front of the forehead.

LAZY

Tap the palm of the right *L* hand at the left shoulder several times.

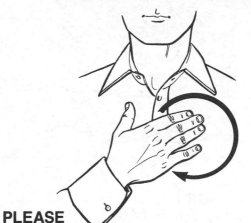

PLEASE

Make a counterclockwise circle with the right flat hand over the heart.

PROUD

With the palm facing down, place the thumb of the right *A* hand against the chest and move the hand straight up.

SMILE

Move the fingers (or just the index fingers) upward and backward across the cheeks from the corners of the mouth.

SURPRISE, AMAZE

Place both closed hands at the temples, with the tips of the index fingers and thumbs touching. Flick both index fingers up at the same time.

UNFAIR

With the palms facing each other, strike the fingertips of the left *F* hand with the fingertips of the right *F* hand in a downward movement.

BLAME, FAULT, MY FAULT, YOUR FAULT

Strike the back of the left closed hand with the little-finger edge of the right A hand. Point the right knuckles and thumb to self or another, depending on who is being referred to.

SHOCK

Circle the eyes with both C hands and suddenly open the hands to a wide C position.

SILLY

Pass the right Y hand rapidly back and forth in front of the forehead a few times. The palm faces left.

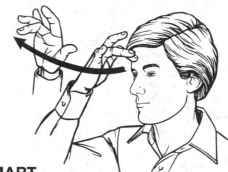

SMART

Touch the forehead with the right middle finger while keeping the other fingers extended. Direct the middle finger outward and upward. The index finger can also be used.

SORRY

Make a few counterclockwise circles over the heart with the right A (or S) hand.

WISH

With the palm facing the body, move the right C hand down the chest from just below the neck.

BOSTON

Place the *B* hand near the right shoulder, with the palm out, and make a downward movement twice.

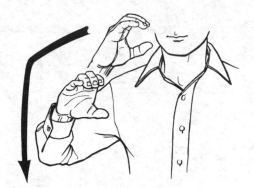

CHICAGO

Move the right *C* hand to the right from just above shoulder level and down a short distance.

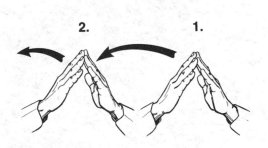

CITY, TOWN

Make the point of a triangle with both flat hands in front of the chest. Repeat a few times while moving the hands to the right.

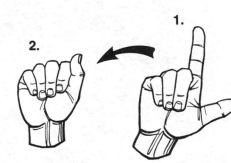

LOS ANGELES

Fingerspell *L* and *A*.

NEW YORK

Place the *Y* hand on the left upturned palm and slide it back and forth.

STATE

Place the index and thumb side of the right *S* hand on the front of the palm-forward left hand, near the top; then move the right hand down in an arc until it rests at the base of the left hand.

ARIZONA
With the palm facing left, slide the thumb of the right
A hand from the right to the left side of the chin.

CALIFORNIA
Touch the right ear with the right index finger; then
move the hand outward and form a *Y* hand with a twist
of the wrist.

Our Fifty States

When the sign for a place-name is not known, it can be fingerspelled. Some
people prefer to fingerspell the abbreviation for state names, such as *P* and *A*
for *Pennsylvania* (PA). Listed below are the names of the fifty states and their
abbreviations. Practice fingerspelling both.

Alabama AL
Alaska AK
Arizona AZ
Arkansas AR
California CA
Colorado CO
Connecticut CT
Delaware DE
Florida FL
Georgia GA
Hawaii HI
Idaho ID

Illinois IL
Indiana IN
Iowa IA
Kansas KS
Kentucky KY
Louisiana LA
Maine ME
Maryland MD
Massachusetts MA
Michigan MI
Minnesota MN
Mississippi MS
Missouri MO
Montana MT

Nebraska NE
Nevada NV
New Hampshire NH
New Jersey NJ
New Mexico NM
New York NY
North Carolina NC
North Dakota ND
Ohio OH
Oklahoma OK
Oregon OR
Pennsylvania PA
Rhode Island RI
South Carolina SC
South Dakota SD

Tennessee TN
Texas TX
Utah UT
Vermont VT
Virginia VA
Washington WA
West Virginia WV
Wisconsin WI
Wyoming WY

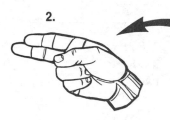 

OHIO
Fingerspell *O* and *H*.

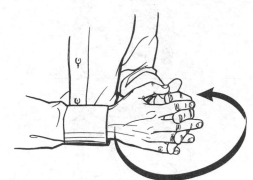

AMERICA
Interlock the fingers of both slightly curved open hands and move them from right to left in an outward circle.

CANADA
Grasp the right jacket or coat lapel (or an imaginary one) and shake it.

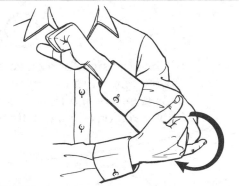

COUNTRY (nation)
Rub the palm side of the right *Y* hand in a counterclockwise direction on the underside of the left forearm near the elbow.

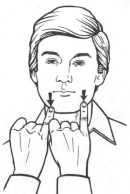

ISRAEL
With the palm side of the right *I* finger, stroke downward on either side of the chin.

MEXICO
Draw the right extended *M* fingertips downward over the right cheek a few times.

LOCATION & DIRECTION 16

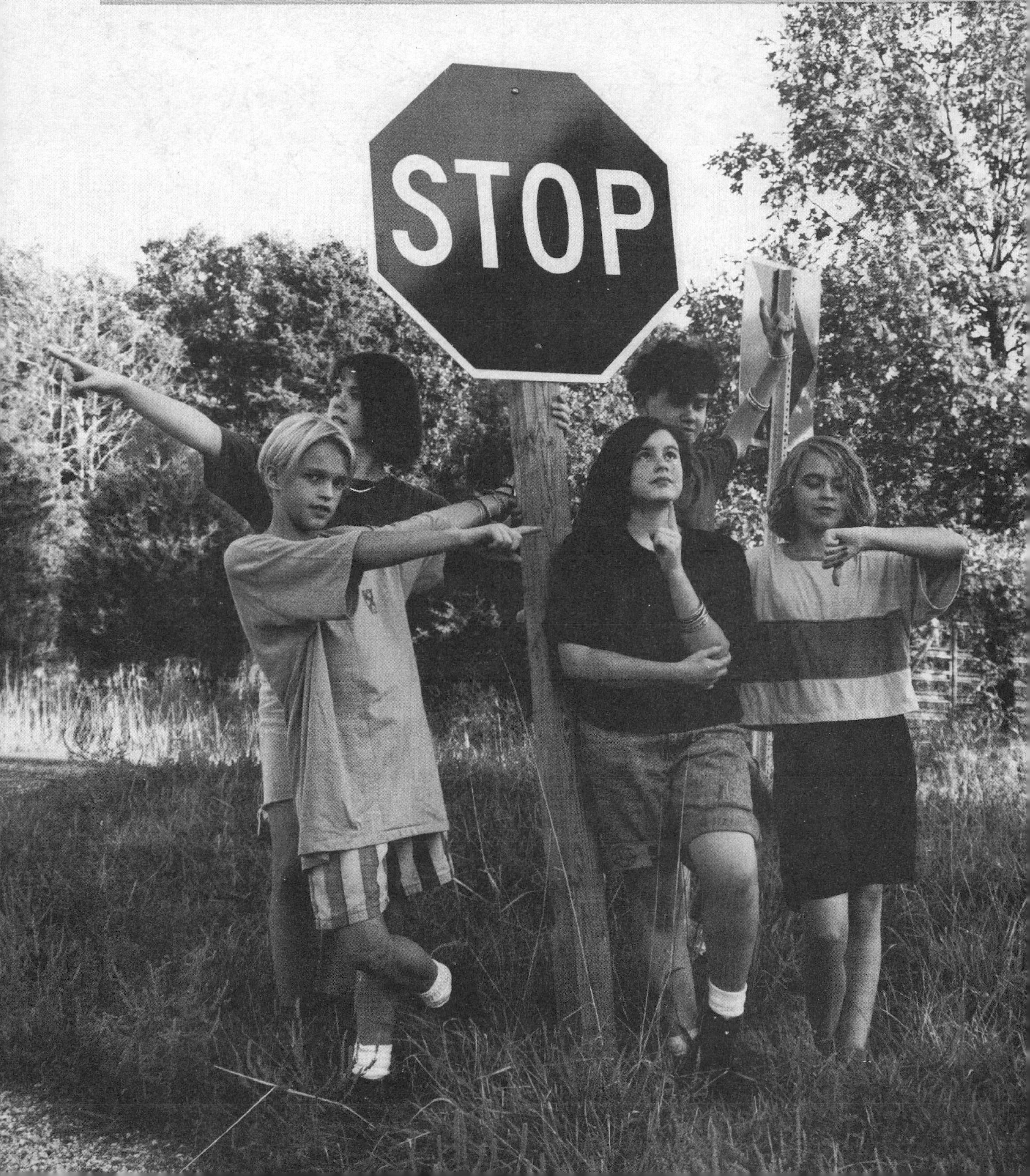

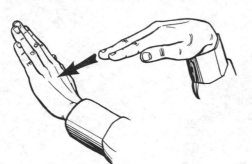

AT
Bring the fingers of the right flat hand in contact with the back of the left flat hand. This sign is often fingerspelled.

BEFORE (location), IN FRONT OF
Hold the left flat hand at eye level with the palm facing in. Move the right flat hand upward with a sweeping motion until the palms face each other.

BEHIND
Hold both *A* hands together, with the palms facing each other. Move the right hand backward behind the left.

BETWEEN
Put the little-finger edge of the right flat hand between the thumb and index finger of the left flat hand. Move the right hand back and forth while keeping the little-finger edge of the right hand in place.

HERE
Hold both flat hands to the front with the palms facing up. Make forward semicircles in opposite directions.

ON
With both palms facing down, place the right flat hand on the back of the left flat hand.

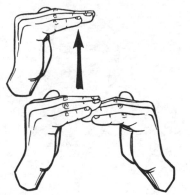

ABOVE, OVER
Hold both bent hands to the front of the body, with the right fingers on top of the left fingers. Raise the right hand a short distance.

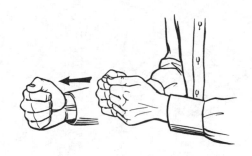

AHEAD
Hold both A hands together, with the palms facing each other. Move the right hand in front of the left.

BELOW, UNDER
Hold both bent hands to the front of the body, with the left fingers on top of the right fingers. Lower the right hand a short distance.

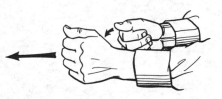

FOLLOW, CHASE
Place both A hands to the front of the body, the left slightly ahead of the right. Move them forward, the right hand following the left. *Chase* is signed more rapidly than *follow*.

FROM
Touch the upright left index finger with the knuckle of the right X-hand index finger; then move the right hand in a slight backward-downward arc.

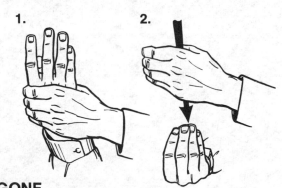

GONE
Draw the right open hand down through the left C hand; end with the right hand in the *and* position below the left hand.

AWAY
Move the right curved hand away from the body and to the right; end with the palm facing forward and down. Sometimes the *A* hand is used at the beginning of the sign.

WHERE
Hold up the right index finger with the palm facing forward, and shake the finger rapidly back and forth from left to right.

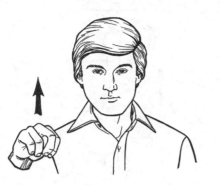

NORTH

Move the right *N* hand up with the palm facing forward.

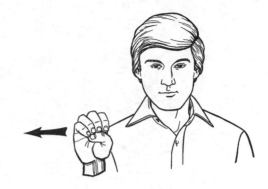

EAST

Move the right *E* hand to the right with the palm facing forward.

SOUTH

Move the right *S* hand down with the palm facing forward.

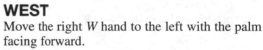

WEST

Move the right *W* hand to the left with the palm facing forward.

UP

With the palm facing forward, hold up the right index finger and move it up a little.

DOWN

With the palm facing in, point the right index finger down and move it down a little.

IN
Move the closed fingers of the right hand into the left *C* hand.

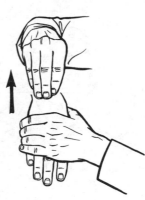

OUT
Place the downturned fingers of the open right hand in the left *C* hand, with the right fingers extending below the left hand. Draw the right hand up and out forming an *and* hand.

RIGHT (direction)
Move the right *R* hand toward the right.

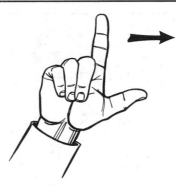

LEFT (direction)
Move the right *L* hand toward the left.

THERE
Point with the right index finger when being specific. For a more general reference, move the right flat hand to the right with the palm facing forward.

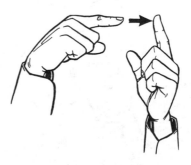

TO
Hold the left index finger up and move the right index finger toward it until the fingertips touch.

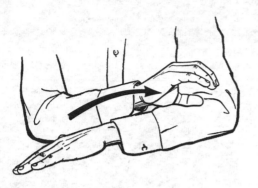

COMPUTER (alternative)

Place the thumb of the right *C* hand on the back of the horizontal left flat hand and move it up the left arm in an arc. (See page 111 for another sign for *computer*.)

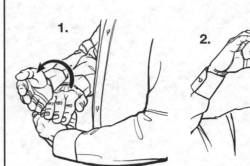

LAPTOP, NOTEBOOK COMPUTER

Place right flat hand on left flat hand, fingers pointing in opposite directions; twist right hand up while still making contact with right little finger on left. Move right *C* hand in a double arc in front of forehead.

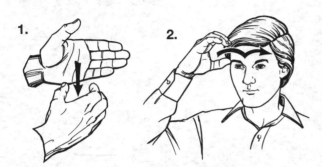

PALMTOP COMPUTER, HANDHELD COMPUTER

Move the thumb and fingertips of right *C* hand down across the left flat palm. With right *C* hand, make a double arc in front of forehead from right to left.

DISPLAY SCREEN, SCREEN, FLAT PANEL SCREEN

Place index fingers side by side and pointing forward in front of the chest with palms down. Draw a rectangle by moving the hands to the sides, down and in.

KEYBOARD

Fingerspell *K-B*. Sign each letter near the right shoulder.

MOUSE

Brush the right index finger to the left across the nose tip twice. *Note:* This sign is also used for the animal *mouse*.

DISK

Place the right *D* hand, palm down with index finger pointing forward, on the left flat hand which has its palm up, and circle twice.

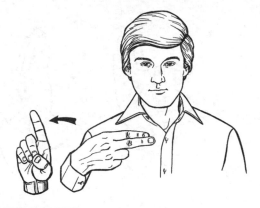

HARD DRIVE

Fingerspell *H-D*. Sign each letter near the right shoulder.

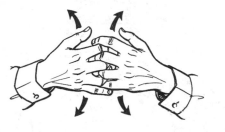

HARDWARE, MACHINE, ENGINE, MOTOR

Join the fingers of both curved open hands in front of the body and move the hands up and down a few times. *Note: Hardware* can be fingerspelled *H-W*.

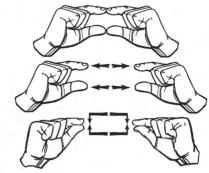

CHIP (computer)

Hold both *Q* hands in front of the body with fingertips touching and outline the shape of a *chip* by moving the hands apart a couple of inches and closing the thumb and index finger.

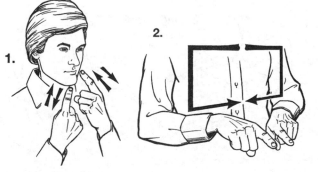

DIALOG BOX

Move both index fingers back and forth from the lips alternately. Place index fingers side by side in front of the chest, palms down and pointing forward. Draw a square by moving hands to the sides, down and in.

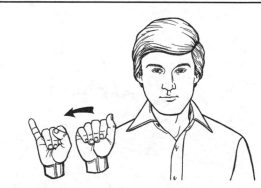

ARTIFICIAL INTELLIGENCE

Fingerspell *A-I*. Sign each letter near the right shoulder

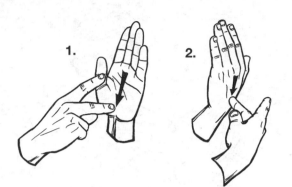

PROGRAM, APPLICATION
Move middle finger of right *P* hand down left flat palm; then twist left hand slightly and move middle finger of right *P* hand down back of left hand.

SOFTWARE
Fingerspell *S-W.* Sign each letter near the right shoulder.

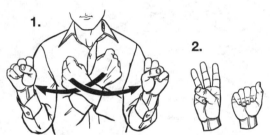

FREEWARE, SHAREWARE
Cross the closed hands on the chest with palms facing in; then rotate them to the sides with palms facing forward. Then fingerspell *W-A-R-E.* Sign each letter near the right shoulder.

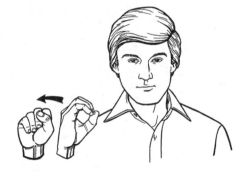

OPERATING SYSTEM, OS
Fingerspell *O-S.* Sign each letter near the right shoulder.

UPGRADE
Move the little-finger edge of the right flat hand in small arcs up the left arm.

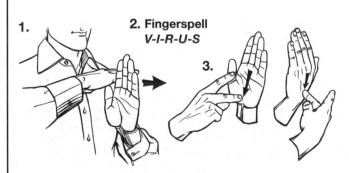

ANTI-VIRUS PROGRAM
Place right flat downturned hand against left flat vertical hand; move hands forward. Fingerspell *V-I-R-U-S.* Next, move middle finger of right *P* hand down left flat palm; then twist the left hand slightly and move middle finger of right *P* hand down back of left hand.

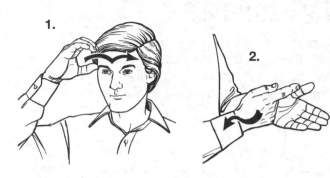

COMPUTER GRAPHICS

Move the right *C* hand, palm left, across the forehead in a double arc from right to left. Hold both hands in front and draw a wavy line with the little-finger side of the right *G* hand over the left flat palm.

PULL DOWN MENU

Place the little-finger edge of the bent right hand on the fingers of the left flat hand. Move the right hand down the left hand in several short arcs.

DATA, INFORMATION

Place the fingertips of both *and* hands on each side of the forehead, then move them forward and down to open hands with palms facing up.

CLICK

Point the right index finger forward and bend it down.

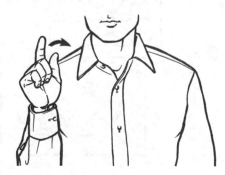

CURSOR

Hold up the modified *G* hand in front of the right shoulder, palm angled forward, and pivot the hand and arm a couple of inches to the left.

Hidden Message

Draw a straight line between each pair of dots with the same letters. The lines will go across only the signs that are part of the hidden message. Write the name of the each of these signs below to discover the hidden message. Answer is at bottom of page.

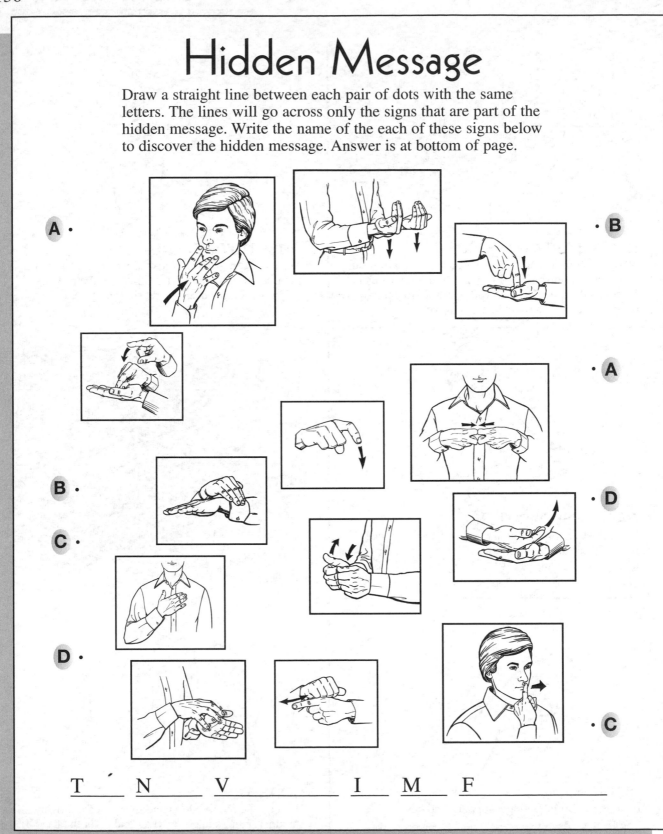

T ´ N V I M F

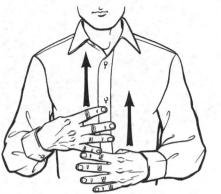

SCROLL

Place both *4* hands in front of the body, right over left, with right little finger on left index and palms in, fingers pointing in opposite directions; move both *4* hands up together a short distance two times.

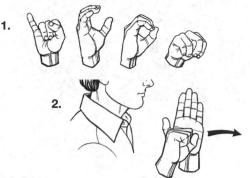

ICON

Fingerspell *I-C-O-N.* Sign each letter near the right shoulder. Sign *symbol* by placing the right *S* hand, palm forward, on the palm of the left flat hand, palm right, and move them forward a little.

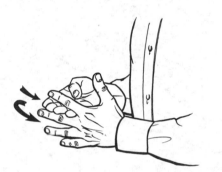

FILE

Slide the palm-up right *B* hand between the index and middle fingers then between the middle and ring fingers of the left open hand, palm in.

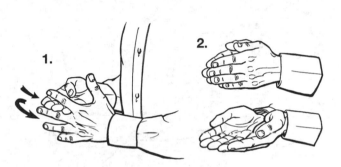

FILE FOLDER, FOLDER

Slide the right *B* hand between the index and middle fingers then between the middle and ring fingers of the left open hand. Place hands palm to palm; open both hands while keeping contact with little fingers.

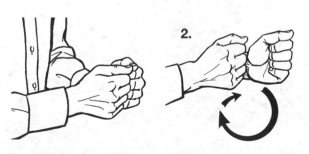

BACKUP

Hold both *A* hands side by side in front of the body. Move the right *A* hand in an arc down, back and forward until it touches the heel of the left hand.

GLITCH

Touch the bent knuckles of both *U* (or *V*) hands together and twist them back and forth in opposite directions.

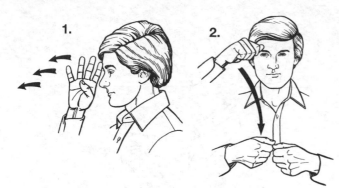

VIRTUAL MEMORY

Touch the right *4* hand at the right side of the fore-head, palm facing left. Move the right hand forward in several short movements. Place the thumb of right *A* hand on forehead; then on top of left *A*-hand thumb.

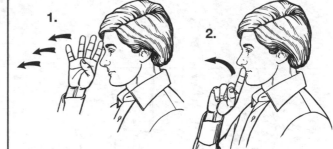

VIRTUAL REALITY

Touch the right *4* hand at the right side of the fore-head, palm facing left. Move the right hand forward in several short movements. With palm facing left, move the right index finger in a forward arc from the lips.

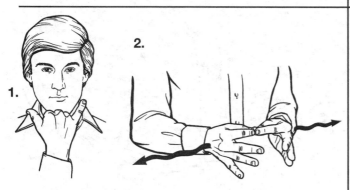

ERROR MESSAGE

Place the *Y* hand on the chin with the palm facing in. Touch the thumb and index fingers of both *F* hands in front of the chest. Pull the hands apart to the sides, either with a wavy or straight motion.

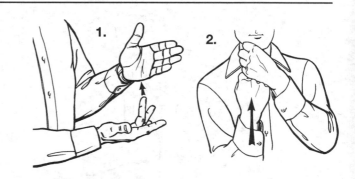

TECHNICAL SUPPORT

Tap the tip of the bent palm-up-middle finger of the right open hand twice on the little-finger edge of the left flat hand, palm right. Bring right *S* hand up under left *S* hand and move hands up a short distance.

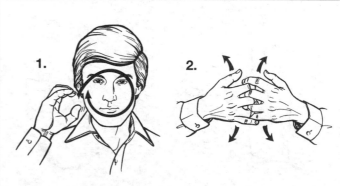

TEXT, SENTENCES

Touch the thumb and index fingers of both *F* hands in front of the chest. Pull the hands apart to the sides, either with a wavy or straight motion.

SEARCH ENGINE

Make a few circular motions across the face from right to left with the right *C* hand, palm left. Then join the fingers of both curved open hands in front of the body and move the hands up and down a few times.

ENCRYPTION

Place the left curved open hand in front with palm facing up. Circle the right curved open hand above the left.

PASSWORD, ACCESS CODE

Place the right *A* thumb over the lips a few times. Next, hold the left index finger up with palm facing right; then place the thumb and index finger of the right *Q* hand against it.

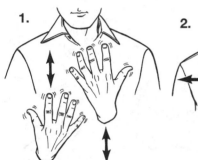

FIREWALL

Move slightly curved open hands up and down alternately in front of body while wiggling fingers. Touch *B* hands in front, palms out, and move them apart together stopping in front of shoulders.

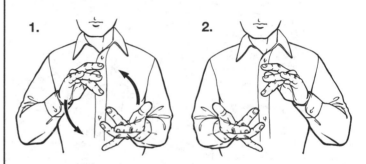

INTERNET, THE NET

Hold both open hands in front with bent middle fingers facing each other. Then twist the hands to switch positions.

BLOG (to journal/diary on the internet)

Fingerspell *B-L-O-G.* Sign each letter near the right shoulder.

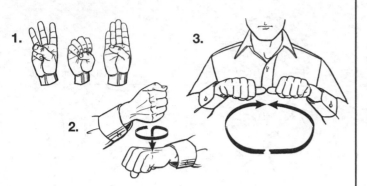

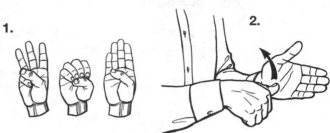

WEB SITE

1. Fingerspell *W-E-B*. 2. Circle right *A* hand above left closed hand; place right *A* hand on left. 3. Touch thumbs of *A* hands together a short distance in front. Circle hands toward self and touch thumbs again near chest.

WEB PAGE

Fingerspell *W-E-B*. Sign each letter near the right shoulder. Move the extended thumb of the right *A* hand upward as it strikes the open palm of the left hand twice.

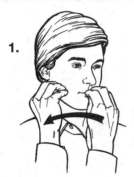 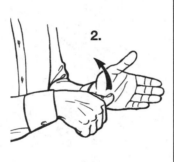

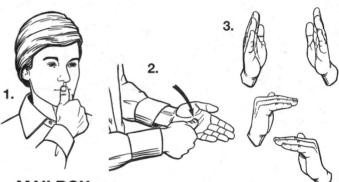

HOME PAGE

Place the fingertips of the right *and* hand first at the mouth, then at the right cheek. Move the extended thumb of the right *A* hand upward as it strikes the open palm of the left hand twice.

MAILBOX

Place right *A* thumb on mouth, then on palm of the upturned left hand. Next, point fingertips of both flat hands up with palms facing each other in front of body. Bend both hands with the right hand over left.

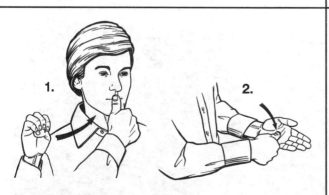

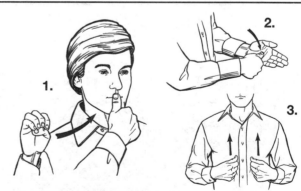

E-MAIL (Electronic Mail)

Fingerspell *E* near the right shoulder. Next, place the right *A* thumb on the mouth and then on the palm of the upturned left hand.

E-MAIL ADDRESS

Fingerspell *E* near the right shoulder. Next, place the right *A* thumb on the mouth and then on the palm of the upturned left hand. Then move the palm sides of both *A* hands up from the abdomen to the chest.

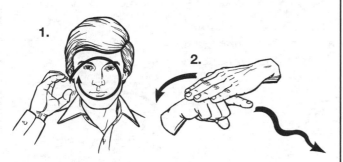

SURF, SURF THE NET

Make a few circular motions across face from right to left with right *C* hand, palm left. Move right index finger forward in a wavy movement from under left flat hand as left flat palm moves up right arm.

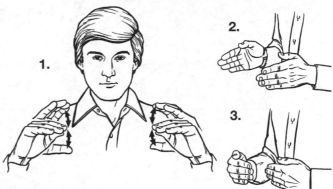

CHAT ROOM

Place both flattened *C* hands at sides of chest, palms facing. Close and open them together a couple of times. Place flat hands in front, palms facing; move left hand near body and right hand in front, palms facing body.

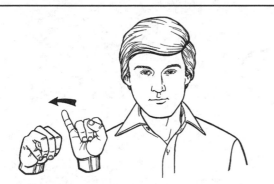

IM (Instant Messaging)

Fingerspell *I-M* near the right shoulder.

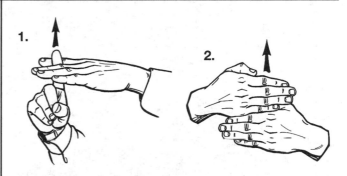

POP-UP WINDOW

With palm left, move right index finger upward between index and middle fingers of left flat hand, palm down. Place right flat hand on left flat hand with palms in. Move right hand up a short distance.

SPAM (unwanted e-mail)

Fingerspell *S-P-A-M*. Sign each letter near the right shoulder.

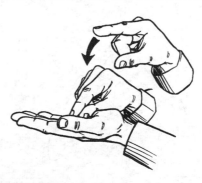

PRINTER (machine)

Move the right index finger and thumb together as though picking something up; then place them on the left flat palm.

What Sign Is It?

Below are signs from previous chapters. Write the answer in the box under each sign. Answers are at bottom of page.

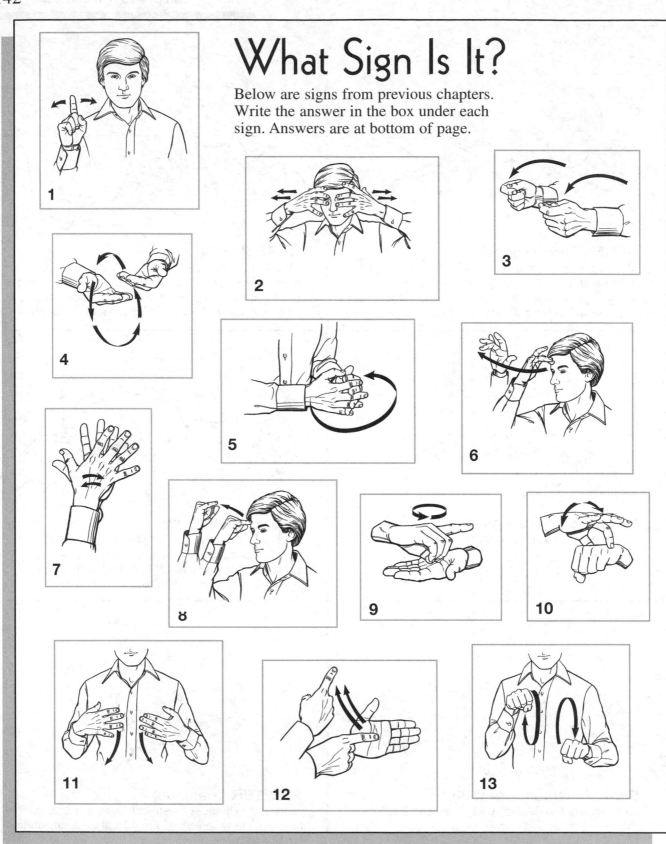

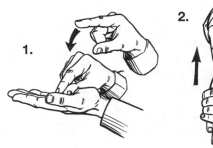
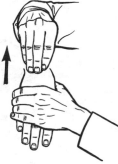
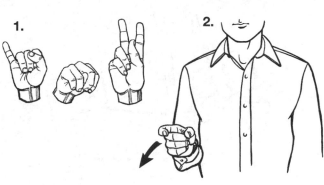

PRINTOUT

Move right index finger and thumb together as if picking something up; place them on left flat palm. Hold downturned fingers of open right hand in left C hand. Pull right hand up and out forming an *and* hand.

INK CARTRIDGE

Fingerspell *I-N-K* near the right shoulder. Move the right curved *L* fingers forward several inches in front of the chest.

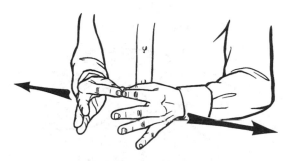

CABLE

Hold both C hands to the front with palms down and hands touching. Move the right hand away from the left hand to the right side in a wavy motion.

CAPTION, CAPTIONING

Place both *F* hands together in front and touching, palms facing, and pull them apart together to the sides in a straight line two times.

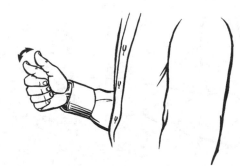
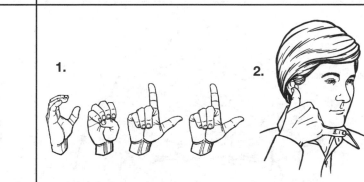

REMOTE CONTROL

Point the extended right *A* hand thumb forward, palm left, and move the thumb up and down a few times.

CELL PHONE

Fingerspell *C-E-L-L* near the right shoulder. Then place the *Y* hand at the right side of the face with the thumb near the ear and the little finger near the mouth.

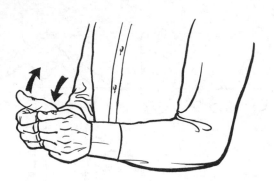

VIDEO GAME
Hold both *A* hands to the front and side by side and alternately move the thumbs up and down.

JOYSTICK
Place the right *S* hand in the left flat palm which is facing up. Swivel the right *S* hand in several directions, such as forward, backward and side to side a few times.

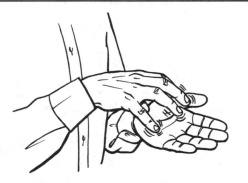

CALCULATOR
Hold the right curved open hand over the left flat palm which faces up, and wiggle the bent fingers of the right hand near the left palm.

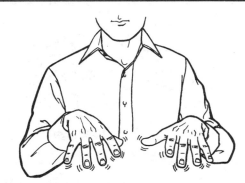

TYPE, TYPEWRITER
Place both open hands in front of the body, palms down, and alternately wiggle the fingers as if typing. To sign *typewriter*, move the hands alternately up and down a couple of times.

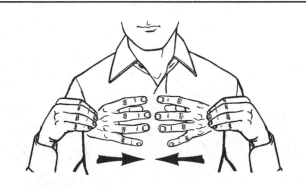

MICROWAVE
Place both flat *O* hands facing each other and to the sides of the chest. Throw the hands towards each other while changing them to curved open hands twice.

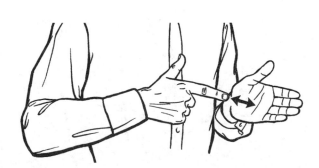

LASER, BURN
Point the right *L*-hand index finger at the left flat-hand palm and move the right *L* hand back and forth twice.

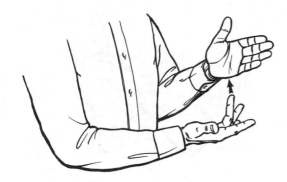

TECHNOLOGY, TECHNICAL

Tap the tip of the bent palm-up-middle finger of
the right open hand twice on the little-finger edge
of the left flat hand, palm right.

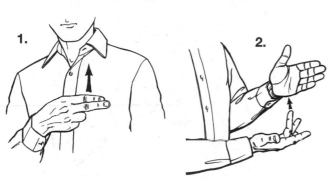

HIGH-TECH

Raise the *H* hand in front of the chest with palm
facing in. Tap the tip of the bent palm-up-middle
finger of the right open hand twice on the little-finger
edge of the left flat hand, palm right.

SATELLITE

Circle the right *S* hand around the left *S* hand.

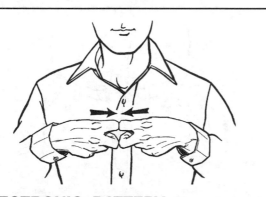

ELECTRONIC, BATTERY

Strike the bent index and middle fingers of each hand
(or just the index fingers) together a few times. The
other fingers are closed. *Note:* This is also the sign
for *electricity*, see page 111.

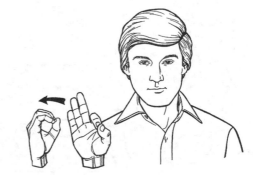

FIBER OPTICS

Fingerspell *F-O* near the right shoulder.

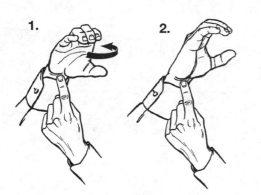

RADAR

Place the base of the right *C* hand, palm forward, on the upturned left *one* fingertip, palm in, and turn the *C* hand in towards the body.

VIDEO

Place the thumb side of the right open hand on the left flat palm which faces right and points up, and wiggle the fingers.

ROBOT

Place flat hands at each side, right hand higher than left, and move the arms up and down alternately like a *robot*. *Note:* Some move the legs and arms alternately up and down.

MAGNET, MAGNETIC

With palms down, place both *M* hands to the front of the chest and a few inches apart; pivot the hands towards each other until the index fingers (or fingertips) touch once or twice

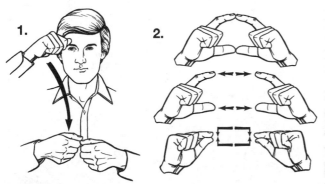

MEMORY CARD

Place thumb of right *A* hand on forehead; then place it on left *A*-hand thumb. Touch fingertips of both bent *L* hands in front of chest with palms forward. Pull hands apart to sides, stop and close index fingers and thumbs.

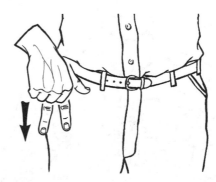

PAGER

Place the right *S* hand in front of the right side of the hip and thrust the thumb, index and middle fingers (*3* hand) down together once or twice.

MISC. SIGNS 18

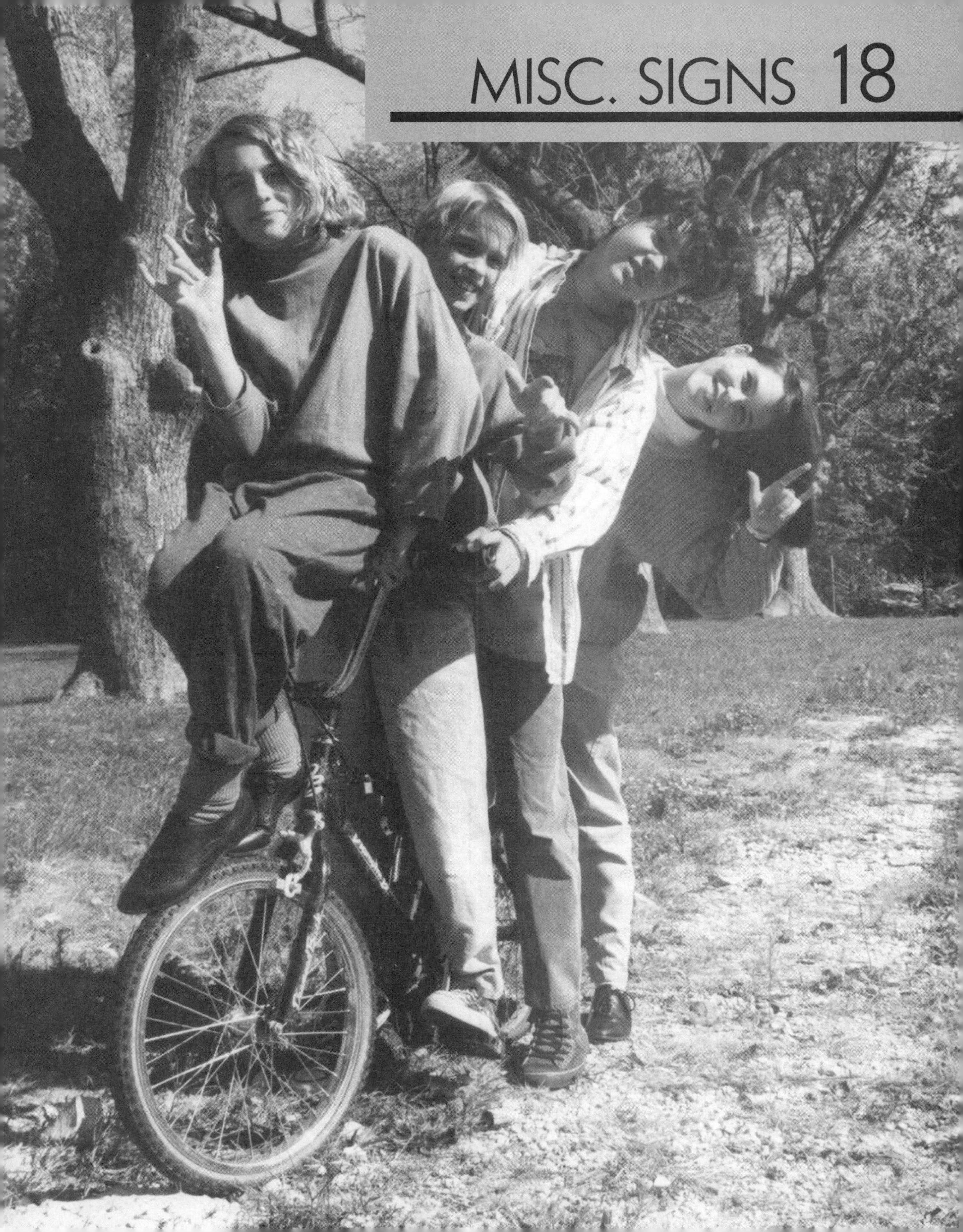

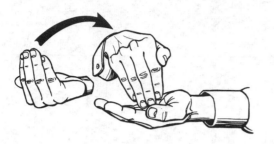

AGAIN, REPEAT

Hold the left flat hand pointing forward, palm up, and the right bent hand palm up. Move the right hand upward and over until the fingertips touch the left palm.

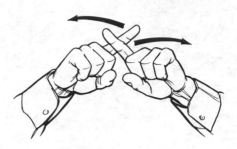

BUT

With the palms facing out, cross both index fingers; then draw the fingers apart a short distance.

ENVY

Place the tip of the right index finger between the teeth and move slightly from side to side a few times.

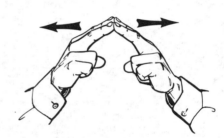

VERY

With the palms facing in, touch the fingertips of both *V* hands; then draw both hands apart to the sides.

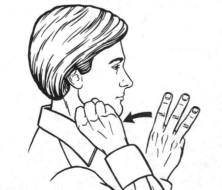

WAS

Hold the right *W* hand in front of the body, with the palm facing left. Move the hand backward to the side of the neck or cheek, and at the same time change from a *W* to an *S* hand.

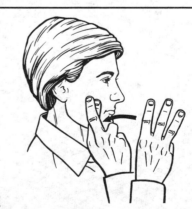

WERE

Hold the right *W* hand slightly to the front of the body, with the palm facing left. Move the hand backward to the side of the neck or cheek, and at the same time change from a *W* to an *R* hand.

AND

Place the right open hand in front of the body, with the palm facing in and the fingers pointing to the left. Move the hand to the right while bringing fingertips and thumb together.

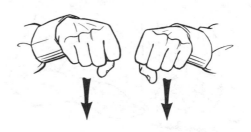

CAN

Hold both *S* (or *A*) hands in front of the body and move them down firmly together.

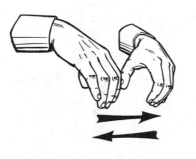

DO

Point both *C* hands down in front of the body and move them at the same time, first to one side and then the other.

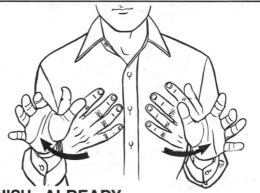

FINISH, ALREADY

Hold both open hands to the front with the palms facing the body and the fingers pointing up. Shake the hands quickly out to the sides a few times.

THAT

Place the right downturned *Y* hand on the left upturned palm.

WHICH

With the palms facing each other, move the *A* hands alternately up and down in front of the chest.

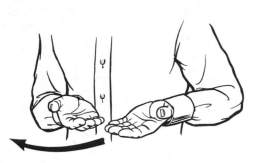

BRING

Hold both open hands to the front with the palms facing up and one hand slightly in front of the other. Move both hands toward self or another person, or to the right or left, depending on who is indicated.

CARRY

Hold both slightly curved hands to the front with the palms facing up. Move both hands at the same time in an arc from right to left.

DON'T, NOT

Place the right *A* thumb under the chin and move it forward and away from the chin.

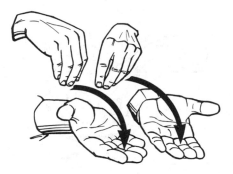

GIVE

Hold both *and* hands to the front with the palms facing down. Move the hands forward, and at the same time form flat hands with the fingers pointing forward and the palms facing up.

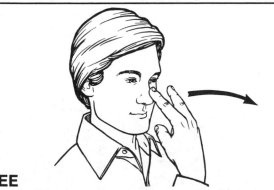

SEE

With the palm facing in, place the fingertips of the right *V* hand near the eyes and move the right hand forward.

THANKS, THANK YOU, YOU'RE WELCOME

Touch the lips with the fingertips of one or both flat hands; then move the hands forward until the palms are facing up. It is natural to smile and nod the head while making this sign.

KEEP

Cross the wrist of the right *V* hand over the wrist of the left *V* hand.

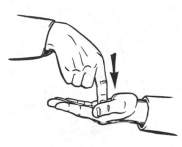

THIS

Put the tip of the right index finger into the palm of the left flat hand.

WHAT

Pass the tip of the right index finger down over the left flat hand from the index to the little finger.

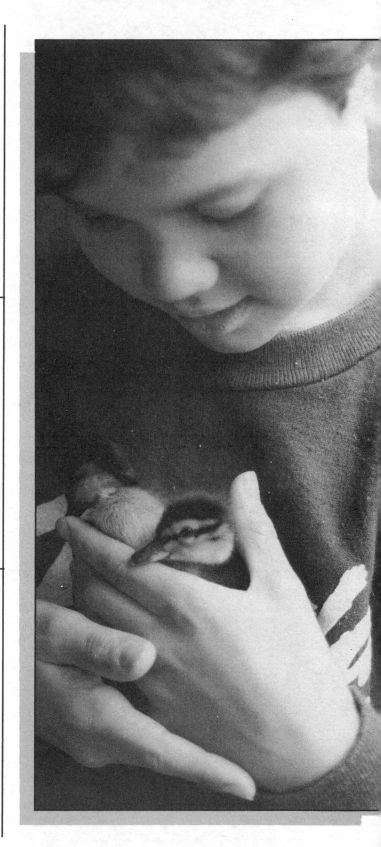

AM, ARE, BE, IS

Place the thumb of the right *A* hand on the lips and move the right hand forward. Make the same movement and initialize as follows: for *are* use *R*; for *be* use *B*; and for *is* use *I*.

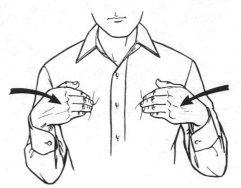

HAVE

Place the fingertips of both bent hands on the chest.

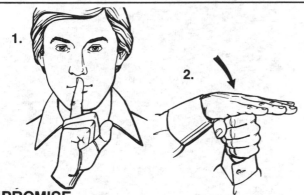

PROMISE

Touch the lips with the right index finger; then move the right flat hand down and slap it against the thumb and index-finger side of the left closed hand.

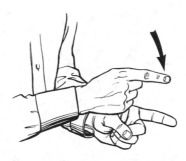

RIGHT, CORRECT

Point both index fingers forward and bring the little-finger edge of the right hand down onto the thumb edge of the left hand.

SMELL

Pass the slightly curved palm of the right hand upward in front of the nose a few times.

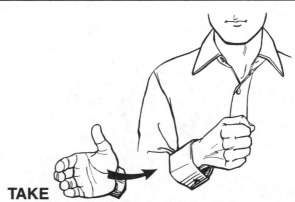
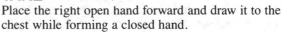

TAKE

Place the right open hand forward and draw it to the chest while forming a closed hand.

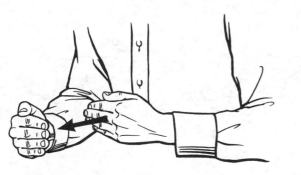

AFTER

Hold the left slightly curved hand out to the front with the palm facing in. Place the right curved palm on the back of the left hand and move it forward and away from the left hand.

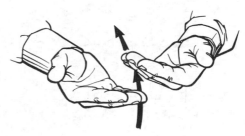

ALMOST

Brush the little-finger edge of the right hand upward over the fingertips of the left curved hand. Both palms face up.

ASK

Bring both flat hands together so that the palms touch, and move them in a backward arc toward the body.

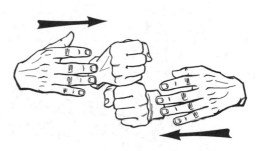

GET, RECEIVE

Bring both open hands together while forming *S* hands, and place the right on top of the left. The hands can be moved toward the body, especially when signing *receive*.

RULES

Place the right *R* hand on the front of the palm-forward left hand, near the top; move the right hand down in an arc to the base of the left.

TOGETHER

Place the knuckles of both *A* hands together and move them in a forward semicircle to the left.

POSTER

With the palms facing forward, hold up both index fingers and outline a square.

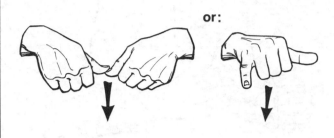

STAY

Place the tip of the right *A* thumb on top of the left *A* thumb and move both hands down together.
Alternative: Move the right *Y* hand down a short distance.

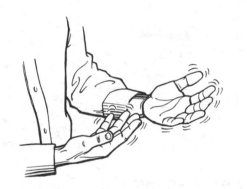

WAIT

With the palms facing up, hold up both curved open hands to the left, the right hand behind the left. Wiggle all the fingers.

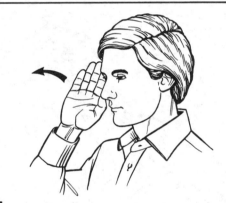

WILL

Place the right flat hand opposite the right temple or cheek, with the palm facing in. Move the hand straight ahead.

WITH

Join the two *A* hands, with the palms facing each other.

FANTASTIC, GREAT

Push both flat open hands forward and up several times with palms facing out.

FAVORITE
Tap the chin a few times with the right middle finger.

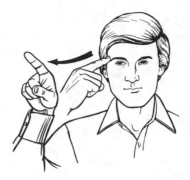

FOR
Touch the right temple with the right index finger; then dip it forward until the finger points forward.

MEET
Bring both *D* hands together from the sides, with the palms facing each other.

QUESTION
Use the right index finger to outline a question mark in the air. Be sure to include the dot underneath.

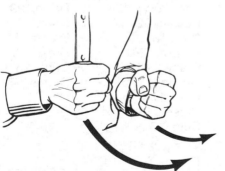

TRY
Hold both *S* hands (or *T* hands) to the front with palms facing each other; then move hands forward with a pushing motion.

WHY
Touch the forehead with the fingers of the right hand; then move the hand forward while forming the *Y* hand with the palm facing in.

Index

Available wherever books are sold

SIGNING IS FUN by Mickey Flodin

From the premiere publishers of sign language books: a primer for children in grades 1 to 3 that introduces them to the wonders of signing.

THE POCKET DICTIONARY OF SIGNING (Revised Edition) by Rod R. Butterworth and Mickey Flodin

The first easy-to-use pocket reference guide to sign language.

THE PERIGEE VISUAL DICTIONARY OF SIGNING, 3rd Edition by Rod R. Butterworth and Mickey Flodin

This revised and expanded edition is the most comprehensive alphabetized reference work available of American Sign Language.

SIGNING FOR KIDS by Mickey Flodin

For eight- to fourteen-year-olds, an invaluable guide for learning American Sign Language. Illustrated with more than 1,000 signs aimed specifically at kids' interests.

SIGNING ILLUSTRATED: THE COMPLETE LEARNING GUIDE by Mickey Flodin

A complete learning guide that teaches American Sign Language by "category," the most popular and preferred method of teaching and learning.

SIGNING EVERYDAY PHRASES by Mickey Flodin

The easy way to learn basic sign language in English word order for everyday life.

SIGNING MADE EASY by Rod R. Butterworth, M.A., M.Ed., and Mickey Flodin

A complete program for learning sign language. Includes drills and exercises for increased comprehension and signing skills.

PERIGEE

An imprint of Penguin Group (USA) Inc.

penguin.com